Praise

"Moving, thoughtful, and a ~~heart-centered guide~~de for the journey that each of us must undertake."

—Jerry Colonna, author of *Reboot* and *Reunion*

"Through Ben's visceral and honest storytelling, we remember what it means to be alive, to go deep within ourselves when we have no idea what we will find."

—Kaitlin B. Curtice, award-winning
author of *Native* and *Living Resistance*

"Practical, compassionate, and poignant. . . . The go-to guide for the next generation of adults approaching midlife."

—Brandan Robertson, author of *Dry Bones & Holy Wars*

"Listen to this vulnerable, daring invitation to embark on your own inner adventure."

—Jesse Israel,
founder of The Big Quiet

"Heartfelt and honest storytelling that's packed with wisdom."

—Scott Shigeoka, author of *SEEK*

"Courageous and vulnerable. . . . A powerfully relevant map for those who have lost their heart."

—Aubert Bastiat, cofounder of Sacred Sons

"A wonderful read for myth-lovers and spiritual adventurers."

—Casper ter Kuile, author of *The Power of Ritual*

THE WAY HOME

THE
WAY
HOME

Discovering the Hero's Journey
to Wholeness at Midlife

BEN KATT

ST. MARTIN'S
ESSENTIALS
NEW YORK

First published in the United States by St. Martin's Essentials, an imprint of St. Martin's Publishing Group

THE WAY HOME. Copyright © 2024 by Ben Katt. All rights reserved. Printed in the United States of America. For information, address St. Martin's Publishing Group, 120 Broadway, New York, NY 10271.

www.stmartins.com

Designed by Steven Seighman

The Library of Congress Cataloging-in-Publication Data is available upon request.

ISBN 978-1-250-91044-8 (trade paperback)
ISBN 978-1-250-91045-5 (ebook)

Our books may be purchased in bulk for promotional, educational, or business use. Please contact your local bookseller or the Macmillan Corporate and Premium Sales Department at 1-800-221-7945, extension 5442, or by email at MacmillanSpecialMarkets@macmillan.com.

First Edition: 2024

10   9   8   7   6   5   4   3   2   1

To Cherie, my muse.

To Evie, Jackson, and Zara:
my life, my grace, my light.

CONTENTS

Many will laugh at my foolishness. But no one will laugh more than I laughed at myself. So I overcame scorn. But when I had overcome it, I was near to my soul, and she could speak to me, and I was soon to see the desert becoming green.

—CARL JUNG, THE RED BOOK

I did not ask for success; I asked for wonder. And you gave it to me.

—RABBI ABRAHAM JOSHUA HESCHEL

To realize one's destiny is a person's only obligation.

—PAULO COELHO, THE ALCHEMIST

LANGUAGE OF THE JOURNEY

Since a new journey often requires not only learning new concepts, but also embracing a fresh vocabulary to experience those concepts, I've created this list (1) to familiarize you with ideas that are relevant for your journey, and (2) to provide you with a reference point as you get oriented to the unique terminology from my quest that you will encounter in these pages. Read it when you begin as a teaser for what's ahead, or skip it and come back when you need a refresher for a term.

IF YOU DON'T HAVE YOUR HEART, YOU HAVE NOTHING—The words the voice within spoke to me that began my journey. My Call to Adventure.

CALL TO ADVENTURE—The invitation or summons that begins your departure from the life you've known and initiates the way home.

GRACE, SPACE, PACE—A 1950s Jaguar automobile slogan that inspired me to practice pilgrimage, solitude, and shabbat (a Jewish practice of rest).

MASCOT RULES—Two policies from my brief stint as a mascot that I later realized I expressed in the rest of my life: *Don't speak with your inner voice* and *Don't let people see your true face.*

SOUL—The core, essential you. Your True Self. Who you really are.

EGO—The part of you that gives you a sense of identity and importance. A fragment of who you really are that helps mediate your interaction with the world.

PERSONA—A distorted version of yourself that the ego presents externally to help you fit in and stay safe. Your False Self. I also call this the *Impostor*.

IMPOSTOR—See *Persona*.

SHADOW—Aspects of your identity that you unconsciously reject and repress because you see them as dangerous or bad.

SECOND HALF OF LIFE—The soul-rooted season of life that begins when you discover you've outgrown the egocentric approach to life.

ANAM CARA—Soul friend, from the Irish word *anamchara*. A spiritual companion on the journey home.

KALYANA MITRA—Sanskrit for "spiritual friend." The concept of admirable friendship from Buddhist community life.

POSSESSION-CONTROL-MASTERY—A phrase from Willie James Jennings's *After Whiteness* that I use as shorthand for the selfish and oppressive approach to life that was behind my obsession with producing, perfecting, and performing, and has been so harmful across time and place.

GET QUIET—The words my wife Cherie spoke to me when I was refusing to let go of my old ways of moving through the world.

CROSSING THE THRESHOLD—The moment in the journey where you definitively let go of your old ways and step into the unknown of who you are becoming.

DREAMTIME—A term used by aboriginal Australians to refer to when the Ancestral Spirits created life, which happens in both the past and the present. It is the time when new creative possibilities emerge. As such, I implement the term to capture the mystical experience of transitioning from who you were into who you are becoming.

JAGUAR DREAM—A powerful dream I had that emboldened me to leave the familiar and enter the unknown. It also urged me to become a spiritual student of the jaguar.

SOUL QUEST—A rite of passage ceremony that involves undergoing a spiritual death and marks the transition into a new way of being in the world and participating in community. Inspired by the Indigenous practice of *hanbleceya*, or *vision quest*, which means "crying for a dream." Also referred to as a *wilderness quest*.

BELLY OF THE BEAST—A recurring mythical image that captures the experience of being disoriented in the darkness and experiencing death before being reborn.

DARK NIGHT OF THE SOUL—A phrase from John of the Cross that refers to the experience of feeling disconnected from the divine. More broadly, it describes a painful, difficult season in your life.

OWL ENCOUNTER—The surprise meeting I had with a barred owl during a ritual my friend Vanya facilitated for me in a place that became my *spot of time,* a sacred and rejuvenating place.

ARCHETYPE—A recurring symbol in human consciousness that shows up across myths, stories, and even dreams.

DAD DREAM—The second dream I had in my parents' basement that included layers of meaning and revealed multiple forces of resistance to my growth.

REVERENT, OBEDIENT CADET—A term from my childhood that I use to describe a false part of myself that I needed to discharge so that I could continue to grow into wholeness. My personal version of what Bill Plotkin calls the *Loyal Soldier.*

CIRCLE OF STONES—The location of a spontaneous ceremony where I said thanks and farewell to my reverent, obedient cadet during a day *Wander,* an intentional walk in nature to connect with your soul.

SACRED NAME—A soul name capturing who you truly are and why you're here that you might receive on your journey. And, no, I don't share mine in this book.

CANYON—The site of my soul quest, the capstone experience of my journey to get my heart back.

SAGUARO—The kind of cactus you picture when someone says, "cactus." One of my teachers and healers on my path.

PONDEROSA PINES—The place where I set up camp for my solo fasting experience in the canyon, created a temple, and performed a *Walking Obituary,* a ceremony that enacted my spiritual death.

HUMMINGBIRD—A frequent visitor during my adventure, especially during my experience of solitude and fasting in the canyon.

MAGIC FLIGHT—The often-challenging experience of reemerging from a deep season of self-exploration and integrating your discoveries into everyday life.

X & Y—Letters used by my wilderness quest guides to stand for "ego" and "soul," respectively, as they taught us about how to bring our canyon discoveries back home and live a life in which ego is in service to soul.

MISTER MYSTICAL—The name of the one-man show I performed and my alter ego . . . or perhaps it is my true self?

DONALD DREAM—The visionary dream I had one night in the canyon in which I sang a song to a former President.

MASTER OF THE TWO WORLDS—Joseph Campbell's name for a person who is at once grounded in the magnificence of soul and present in the mundanity of everyday life.

FOLLOW YOUR BLISS—Campbell's catchphrase that refers to living in alignment with your soul.

Tell me, what is it you plan to do with
your one wild and precious life?

—Mary Oliver, "The Summer Day"

Furthermore, we have not even to risk
the adventure alone; for the heroes of all
time have gone before us; the labyrinth
is thoroughly known; we have only to
follow the thread of the hero-path.

—Joseph Campbell,
The Hero with a Thousand Faces

A MILLION WAYS TO LOSE YOUR HEART

There are a million ways to lose your heart.

I'm sure this is true about your actual, physical heart. But what I'm referring to are the countless ways to lose that core, essential you. Your true self. Your identity. Your soul.

There are reckless and rock-bottom ways. Scandalous and selfish ways. Humiliating ways. Illegal ways, too. Losing your heart can be loud and obvious, visible and public. For example, shady or greedy behavior that leads to financial ruin, spiraling into drug or alcohol addiction, the betrayal of a human relationship through an affair, exploitation and abuse, or other choices. And then there are the loud things of life, like violence, disease, and trauma, that can also threaten to devour hearts.

These ways are tragic. But they're not the only ways to lose your heart.

Most of the million ways are actually quiet and ordinary. They happen when everything appears to be just fine on the surface. You can lose your heart while accomplishing good things, accumulating respect, and earning promotions in your career. Or while faithfully fulfilling your duties in relationships—in your marriage, as a son or daughter, as a parent on the sidelines at every soccer game, or as a nice, upstanding citizen in the community. Or you can be in the best shape of your life, be a voracious volunteer, or go to church every Sunday while simultaneously forfeiting your soul . . . forgetting who you are . . . losing your life.

Why is it important to remember that there are also so many quiet ways to lose your heart? Because if you think that losing your heart needs to be dramatic, that it needs to feature a rock-bottom moment that involves something like a mugshot, getting canceled, betraying those you love, or a near-death experience, then you might start to believe that it only happens to *other people*. It's a dangerous thing to believe that only other people lose their hearts. Because it means that you might fail to notice the ordinary, everyday ways your heart is slipping away . . . *in this very moment.*

So many people are losing their hearts right now, whether they realize it or not. Beneath the supposedly satisfactory surface conditions of "ordinary" lives, so many of us aren't okay—particularly men, and especially in midlife. We are grappling with anxiety and lost in loneliness. We're distracted. We're burned out or bored, with no passion or purpose. The lives we've built and the achievements we've pursued have left us disappointed, disillusioned, and depressed. And no partner or promotion or paycheck seems to be able to fix it for us.

We've fallen asleep at the wheel of our own lives.

And we're not quite sure how to wake up.

We need to find a way.

This is what happened to me, and it's what this book is about: losing your heart and finding the way to get it back.

The Motions of Midlife

I was in my early thirties, entering midlife. I had a solid marriage and a rapidly growing family—three kids in three years, while my wife Cherie was also completing graduate school. I was in good health, had a nice house, and enjoyed plenty of meaningful friendships. And, perhaps most importantly to me at the time, I was accomplished in my career, having started three scrappy, community-focused startups that were positively impacting people's lives.

Everything was proceeding according to plan.

It was a nice life. But I couldn't see that there was another side to the story. In poker terms, I felt like I was holding a full house, but I didn't realize that the deck was stacked against me, featuring near perfect conditions for losing my heart. I was cornered by my own lifestyle, with its commitments of career and kids, marriage and mortgage, and other midlife concerns. With my past obligations and future ambitions, I was too busy to be attuned to my heart in the present.

In hindsight, there were signs that my heart was slipping away. Increased fatigue at work. Going through the motions in relationships. Becoming more distant from Cherie and the kids. Like the aging Bilbo Baggins of Tolkien's Middle-earth, I felt "thin, sort of stretched, like butter scraped over too much bread." But there was nothing obvious or dramatic or explosive about it. I was still showing up for work, going on family vacations, and smiling in our annual holiday card (when we were organized enough to send one out).

While all the nice and normal things of my midlife were going on, somewhere along the way, my heart decided to switch off the lights and sneak out the back door.

I never even noticed.

Until one day, midway along the journey of my life, I received a wake-up call and I stumbled upon the road to getting my heart back.

The path to healing and wholeness.

The way home.

And I learned that while there are a million ways to lose your heart, there is only one way to get it back.

It is an ancient way, well-known but less-traveled.

This book is about that way.

If You Don't Have Your Heart

One rainy fall morning I was charging up a hill near the end of a jog. Any other day I would dash around the corner and sprint the last ten blocks to my house. But this day was different. When I reached the top of the hill, my legs burning and music blasting in my ears, a string of words from within suddenly interrupted me.

"If you don't have your heart, you have nothing," the inner voice said.

It stopped me dead in my tracks. Breathing deeply, I pulled out my blaring earbuds and placed my hands at my sides. I couldn't run anymore. I knew exactly what this voice was telling me, and it wasn't about my heart rate. It was about my soul. In that moment it dawned on me that for a long time I had been slowly and quietly losing my heart amid the ordinary stuff of being human—marriage and family and community and work.

The problem wasn't just that my life was busy and full of commitments.

The bigger issue was *how I was approaching everything.*

It would take years for me to realize this (as the pages of this book will prove!), but for the previous year, the past decade, and probably my entire adulthood, I had been ruled by a three-headed monster: striving after success, pursuing perfection, and constantly seeking the approval of others. I had come to believe that these were the only ways I could earn the love and acceptance of others. The sad but inevitable consequence of chasing after external validation through these things was that I had become estranged from my own internal world, from who I truly am, from my heart.

It's actually pretty remarkable if I think about it: In my work as a social entrepreneur, community organizer, and neighborhood pastor, I had spent nearly a decade coming alongside vulnerable neighbors who were well acquainted with trauma and experiencing some brutal combination of homelessness, addiction, mental illness, and sexual exploitation. My work alleviated suffering and fostered belonging. I helped countless people find their way home. And yet there I was. Lost. Feeling like I didn't belong. And trapped in my own form of suffering. You can't make this stuff up!

At the same time, it also makes a lot of sense that I wasn't receiving for my own life what I was preaching and practicing for others. First, because my line of work was perceived by many to be good and virtuous, and since it didn't offer the dangling carrots of paychecks, promotions, and power, I fooled myself into thinking I was immune to the obsession with achievement, perfection, and performance that dominates so much of our society. I was in the "helping professions," after all! But I was absolutely *in* on the game, the game of looking for fulfillment in some external idea or possession or status or opinion. The trick was that I was just playing the game in my own way.

Second, I failed to see that I was losing my heart *because I wouldn't admit it was possible.* My work brought me to the front lines of trauma. The stories I heard and the wounds I witnessed were unimaginable. It made complete sense that many of these neighbors' lives had spiraled out of control. But my life wasn't that dramatic. No divorce, no death in my immediate family. No illness, no financial hardship, no abuse—not to mention all the oppression I avoided as a white straight male American! But, as I would discover, I did carry my own pain. I just needed to give myself permission to acknowledge it—we all do, no matter how loud or quiet. Because if we don't acknowledge it, we keep sending it on to the next generation, to our communities, and to the world. Pain that is not processed is passed on.

That morning message—*If you don't have your heart, you have nothing*—interrupted all of these false narratives and opened my eyes to my lost heart. On one level, it rattled me enough for me to notice how I was becoming withdrawn in all my relationships and signaled my burnout. At a deeper level, it put a spotlight on my fundamental confusion about *who I am* and *why I am here.*

The inner voice declared that I had a choice to make. I could choose to continue down the achievement-oriented, approval-seeking path, on which I was slowly wasting away. Or I could choose to walk a different way. I could seek after something else—my true self, my soul, my heart. My home.

Million Ways vs. The Way

While the particularities of my experience may have been unique—the rain, the run, the real or imagined voice welling up within me—the choice I was being confronted with was not. It is always and everywhere the same choice.

Between remaining stuck in an identity or role you've outgrown and venturing beyond the familiar into a freer, fuller version of yourself.

Between being constrained by a false, fragmented form of yourself and walking the way home to wholeness.

Between the million ways to lose your heart and the one way to get it back.

Everywhere I look I encounter people wrestling with this choice. To be clear, it is not always front and center. The choice between the million ways and the way is often in the background, behind the presenting issues of relationships and careers, transitions and tragedies, and opportunities and failures.

I stumbled upon signs of the choice just a short time ago on a weekend trip for my brother's fortieth birthday on a mini coach bus filled with a dozen men in midlife as we wound our way through the Kentucky hills from one bourbon distillery to another. The choice was there as we toasted to my brother's resilience, not just surviving the pandemic as a restaurant owner-operator, but also finding new ways to thrive in his personal life. It was there too, as a successful but exhausted doctor en-tertained thoughts—and not for the first time—of what other line of work he could go into. And it showed up as a father of three discussed the challenges of caring for his aging parents through illness until death and the resulting implications for his business venture.

Beyond the Bourbon Trail bus, I've witnessed the choice in the friend growing in awareness of the emotional toll it takes on her to always be trying to make those around her happy, and the coaching client dealing with mounting anxiety who acknowledges he is over-consuming cannabis. And I see it all over the journey of the mother, fresh off a three-month sabbat-ical with her husband and daughter, who is now unable to go back to the corporate world that once defined her, as well as the neighbor who is equally terrified about retiring and not retiring because his identity is so wrapped up in the work he does.

Beneath the surface of all these varied experiences and cir-cumstances is this choice between a life-diminishing path and a life-giving one. And just as the presenting realities are distinct for everyone, so are the identities, roles, and expectations we each need to contend with. My journey to get my heart back required that I shed my addiction to producing, perfecting, and performing, and beneath that, a distorted view of what it means to be a loyal helper. But what a person is attached to can take many shapes. Clinging to fear, security, or shame. Hold-ing on to an insatiable need to be needed. Grasping for power and control. Retreating into passive cowardice. Hiding behind anger. Playing the provider, protector, or peacemaker. And a multitude of attachments that can drag people down the mil-lion ways to lesser lives.

You won't always know what you need liberation from when you begin the journey. That's fine. Whatever form it takes will eventually make itself known. All you need to do is choose to take the way home. And if that's the choice you make, this book is here to help you.

The Way to Get Your Heart Back

So what is this way?

It is an old way that many others before you from across culture, place, and time have traveled. It is a pattern that includes three movements:

Leaving the familiar.
Falling into the unknown.
Rising to wholeness.

Phase one consists of the process of leaving the familiarity of the false version of yourself that you've settled for, whether it be achiever, perfectionist, people-pleaser, victim, control freak, antagonist, escapist, or any other unhealthy, limiting attachment. This is your *Impostor* identity, and whatever form it has taken, it becomes apparent that it no longer fits. This first phase represents the initial interruption, unraveling, and separation from life as you've known it.

Phase two involves falling into the unknown. Unable to depend on the former version of yourself and the world you had constructed, you become vulnerable, confused, and lost. This phase involves a series of confrontations as you must undergo the death of who you thought you were in the struggle to reclaim your heart.

Phase three is the task of rising to wholeness, to your real self. You've recovered your heart, but now you must meet the challenges that come with reintegration into the world of everyday life, relationships, and work. You are reborn—and grateful for it—but need to figure out your new place in the world.

During a six-year period of my life, beginning with that *If you don't have your heart, you have nothing* moment, I traveled on this way. But I didn't discover or invent it. It is an adventure that humans have been embarking on for a long time. Joseph Campbell, the twentieth-century mythologist, was an investigator of this way. In his work *The Hero with a Thousand Faces* and beyond, he looked at myths, sacred texts, folklore, and fairy tales from across cultures and religions and saw a common quest in all these diverse stories, a single story appearing across time and place. He famously called this universal way home to wholeness "The Hero's Journey."

Whether or not you've ever heard of it, you already know this pattern. You've seen it running through old sacred stories and spiritual schools, modern movies and books, and the real life of anyone you've ever met who is living their fullest life. The details are different, but it is the same story. While the journey for each character, real or imagined, features distinct guides, particular challenges, and unique twists and turns, each iteration always expresses the same foundational pattern: *Leaving, Falling, Rising.*

It is the biblical and musical story of Joseph and his amazing technicolor dreamcoat. He is betrayed by his jealous brothers and sold into slavery. But then he rises to power where he uses his wisdom to save Egypt and his brothers from famine.

It is the historical story of Francesco, son of a wealthy merchant, at the beginning of the thirteenth century. His self-indulgent lifestyle is interrupted by visions that lead him to forsake riches. He answers a call to care for the poor and sick, becoming the compassionate one known as St. Francis of Assisi.

It is the fictional story of the Marvel Cinematic Universe's T'Challa, a man who must confront dark family secrets and face his rivals. He evades death with the magical heart-shaped herb, and becomes the worthy Black Panther, King of Wakanda.

It is the true story of my friend Neil, who emerges from a battle with cancer with the courage to end a deteriorating marriage, release his attachment to his identity as a successful doctor, and embrace his calling to creative expression.

Mythical Pattern

This single storyline will run through your life too, if you let it. That is, if you are looking to find your way home. This is what myths have always done. This is why they exist.

To recognize the Mythical Pattern as it unfolds in your quest, it is helpful to understand the nature of myth, which comes from the Greek word *mythos,* meaning "story," "word," or "account."

We tend to have a bit of a confusing relationship with the idea of myth. The term is often used to describe ideas or beliefs or stories that are false, made up, imagined—the earth is flat, unicorns exist, and Marie Antoinette said, "Let them eat cake." It isn't. They don't. She didn't.

Myth, as far as we are concerned in this book, is also used to identify a genre of ancient stories from different cultures and religions. Epics, legends, and sagas. Folktales, fairy tales, and fables.

The problem is that the focus of the first meaning of myth often gets applied to the second. So we start talking about whether or not an ancient story is real or not. *Is it true or false?*, we ask.

But that's not the point. Myths aren't focused on facts, whether in their ancient form like Homer's *The Odyssey,* or as they are passed down in sacred religious texts like the story of Noah's ark, or in their modern movie form like *Lord of the Rings.* Myths are metaphors that convey truths about the human experience to help us grow and change. As they tell stories of creation and origins, of raging battles between the gods, and of encounters with magical creatures, myths always have a more important concern than historical details: to help us become more human.

We could say: *people make myths because myths make people.* People write stories full of symbols to help other people live their fullest lives.

In other words, *myths are maps.* They help us navigate the joys and sorrows, triumphs and failures, and order and chaos of being human. When we are lost. When everything is falling apart. Myths help us find our way home. This is where they claim authority. So, in the deepest sense, myths are real. They are the truest of true!

That is why these stories have the power to call out to us beyond their particular place and time, beyond a specific culture or religious tradition or belief system, to our modern world where they offer comfort, bring disruption, and foster wholeness.

To help you live this universal story in your own unique way, this book harnesses the power of the Mythical Pattern in three ways.

First, we will get glimpses of heroes and scenes from a variety of myths. Because whether it is Odysseus crossing Poseidon's raging sea, Jesus fasting in the wilderness, or Luke landing on the swamp planet Dagobah, these stories have a truth to tell about the process of getting your heart back. The stories I will touch upon range from obscure myths to blockbuster movies, but will especially include content from spiritual traditions—including Christian traditions, since that is the part of the pool I was swimming in for much of my life. Remember, there is no need to *believe* anything about these stories, but I do invite you to *receive* the wisdom they have offered humanity for hundreds, even thousands of years.

Second, I'll be sharing the Mythical Pattern as it unfolded in my quest to get my heart back. *If you don't have your heart you have nothing* was just the beginning. Along the way, I was stalked by a jaguar in my dreams and visited by an owl in the woods. I stood naked before a wise cactus and I wept beneath ponderosa pines. These encounters opened me up and dismantled who I thought I was. They called me to search, to surrender, to be set free. The collection of these stories constitutes my own personal myth. I share it in these pages so you can begin to make your myth!

Third, the contents of this book are organized around the Mythical Pattern of *Leaving, Falling, Rising.* Inspired by the work of Joseph Campbell and guided by my own experience, I mapped out ten distinct tasks spread across these three phases. Along these lines, this book features three sections corresponding to the pattern's phases and ten chapters focusing on the main steps on the journey.

The first three chapters explore the terrain of the Leaving the familiar phase:

Answer the Call
Get Help
Let Go

The middle three chapters represent the Falling into the unknown phase:

Befriend the Darkness
Wander in the Wild
Face Your Death

The third act examines the Rising to wholeness phase:

Return Home
Give Your Gift
Be Still

The tenth step and closing epilogue, *Begin Again,* circles back to where things started and explores how to continue to move through the world with the same openness and curiosity that led to the journey in the first place.

Think of these steps as cairns, stacks of stones placed along hiking trails to let you know you are on the right path. While you may experience the ten steps in the exact sequence they appear in this book, it is just as likely that they occur in some rearranged order. Or simultaneously. Or multiple times in recurring fashion. Be aware that some of these steps may feel minor in your journey while others feel massive. That's okay. It will be different for each person.

And that's how it always is with Mythical Pattern—you walk this *universal* path but in your own *unique* way as you discover how to get back home.

Mystical Presence

The Mythical Pattern is the foundation of this quest. But there are also two other elements that are essential for anyone who embarks on this journey: Mystical Presence and Ritual Practice.

Mystical Presence describes *how* one travels on the path. A posture of openness to mystical experience is essential—and inevitable.

The word *mystical* is used to describe a variety of mysterious experiences that transcend human understanding, such as supernatural encounters, spiritual realities, synchronicities, and signs.

Mystical experiences inspire awe. They are typically characterized by feelings of peace, unity, and joy. They often contain meaning, either literal or symbolic. At the same time, they have an ineffable quality to them—*how* and *what* transpired is hard to put into words. Nevertheless, human beings, creative as we are, have come up with all sorts of words to describe these experiences.

William James, the father of modern psychology, called them simply, "religious experiences."

Bill Wilson, the founder of Alcoholics Anonymous, spoke specifically of his most powerful mystical experience as seeing "a great light."

People talk about transcendence, ecstasy, peak experiences, connection, pure consciousness, oneness, or going beyond the ego.

And when particular plants or mushrooms are involved, people might just say, "wow!"

Just as the language people use for these experiences varies, so does the setting.

A mystical encounter can happen in the mountains or the grocery aisle.

On a park bench or church pew.

During a cross-country road trip or psychedelic trip.

At the birth of a child or death of a parent.

Or in bed—during a dream, or during what feminist Susan Sontag referred to as the oldest resource human beings have available to them for blowing their mind. (In case you didn't catch that, she's talking about sex).

It won't likely happen while scrolling through Twitter on the toilet—but who can say for sure?

Mystical experiences can happen *anywhere*, when everything is in its right place or when everything is falling apart. And they can happen to *anyone*. Embracing Mystical Presence is not reserved for some small, elite group of people. It's not just for some holy hermit hiding out in a cave. It's also not exclusively available to people who *believe* or *don't believe* certain things about God or the universe, or who think they do or don't understand what in fact causes an actual mystical experience.

Many of the major world religions, using a host of different names, say God, with a capital G, is the cause. Or *gods*. Certain strands of the Christian tradition give credit to the Holy Spirit or Holy Ghost. It is "the great" or "the vastness" of the *Tao Te Ching*. To many, it is Mother Earth or Nature. To others, it is the divine, the sacred, the soul, the inner voice, the ancestors. Some call it a Higher Power, a unified consciousness, a metaphysical essence, or simply, grace or magic.

Many speculate that what we identify as supernatural is still strictly natural and material, and our detection of it is just the result of sharpened senses. Others physically locate it in the pineal gland or the gut.

Socrates, the fifth-century-BCE Greek philosopher, talked about the voice of his *daimonion*, or "divine something" that frequently cautioned him when he was about to make a mistake. For Star Wars fanatics it is The Force. Meanwhile, Rev. Otis Moss III calls it the "unknown knowable" and "knowable unknown."

Whatever we call the author or cause of mystical experience, ultimately it is, "Unnameable. It is transcendent of all names," as Joseph Campbell once said in a famous PBS interview with Bill Moyers. Beyond name, beyond term, beyond any form or construct. Nevertheless, in this book, I'll use a variety of names for the unnameable. My hope is that this doesn't trip you up. You are, of course, more than welcome to substitute terms from your vocabulary if it helps.

For this quest, it doesn't matter what you call it. It doesn't matter if you credit the experience to a divine entity, a cosmic coincidence, or brain chemistry. What matters is paying attention, yielding to the experience, and taking the next step. You just need to stay open.

Full disclosure: I began this journey with a significant degree of openness to the mystical. As a former pastor with a so-called Master of Divinity degree, I was used to engaging the spiritual realm. A series of mystical experiences got me into that line of work in the first place! Furthermore, in that role I had the unique privilege of listening to and supporting countless people as they tried to make sense of the varieties of spiritual experiences in their lives. And beyond the extensive personal and vocational experience, I also used to watch a lot of *Unsolved Mysteries* as a kid. So there's that.

But whether this is familiar or uncomfortable territory for you, whether or not you have a religious tradition or spiritual background, know that anyone can cultivate an openness to the mystical because our brains are naturally set up for spiritual awareness and receptive to spiritual signals as Lisa Miller, a groundbreaking researcher of spirituality and the brain, demonstrates in her book *The Awakened Brain*.

We are wired for Mystical Presence.

We might just need to develop our mystical muscles a bit.

This is where Ritual Practices, the third crucial aspect of the way, come in handy.

Ritual Practices

Whether or not you are open to mystical experiences, the truth remains that you can't really control if, when, or how they happen. However, through Ritual Practices—the final ingredient for the journey home—you can create the conditions for recognizing and receiving these experiences. Like any endeavor, such as public speaking, competing in sports, or learning to play a musical instrument, it takes practice to develop your mystical muscles, to strengthen your awakened brain.

Especially when there are so many forms of internal and external resistance to engaging the mystical:

It's irrational. You lunatic!
It's beyond the religious boundaries. You heretic!
It's simpleminded and childish. You fool!
It's dangerous. You're becoming a different person!

But Ritual Practices begin to quiet these voices and prepare you to receive.

Your intuition grows.
You open up to authentic, unmediated spiritual experience—
the way of the mystics!
You welcome playfulness and wonder.
You shed your fears.

Not only do Ritual Practices expand your awareness of the signs and omens that come your way, they also give you the endurance to travel this long road to transformation. While a single mystical moment might awaken you to some true part of your identity, Ritual Practices are what continue the conversation.

Ritual Practices include a variety of technologies that humans across time have implemented to awaken us to the gift of life, to the present moment, to all that we are experiencing:

Spiritual disciplines.

Mindfulness practices.

Rites of passage.

Things like prayer, fasting, yoga, meditation, breathwork, generosity, solitude, ceremony, wandering in nature—any activities that aim to help people experience transformation by accessing a higher or inner power, by encountering God or the true self. They are an exercise regimen for the soul, focused on strengthening and softening inner life for outer life in the world. They help us get our hearts back.

Rites of passage, specifically, have always been used as a tool in helping humans grow up. Communities throughout history have created and passed down rituals in order to symbolize and support human transitions into birth, adulthood, parenthood, marriage, roles and positions, enlightenment, death, and more. That's why they have so much to offer us in these moments of maturing into our full human potential. Like myths, they help us make meaning out of our lives.

To be clear, engaging in Ritual Practices isn't about duty or obligation. It is about building intentional habits in your life that keep you anchored in the storm, calm amid the chaos, and at home with the unknown.

It's also important to note that many Ritual Practices have become more popular recently. Some of them have gotten swallowed up in the global "wellness industry," reportedly valued at over $4.5 trillion, which includes a vast spectrum of "wellness" offerings from fitness programs, nutrition plans, and mindfulness apps to plastic surgery, hair restoration, trips to Bali, and any supplement a TikTok influencer can peddle with a money-back guarantee.

Many of these things that have been lumped together in this so-called "wellness" category can actually impede your journey home. This happens when the presentation of the practice preys on the insecurities of the false self and leaves you feeling small, insufficient, or lacking (This is usually a signal that the practice has been appropriated and commodified). So you have to be discerning.

Additionally, some of these offerings, like psychedelics, ice baths, and breathing techniques, can be powerful ritual tools. Go ahead and experiment, but don't confuse the *tool* with the *terrain* of the quest. While some can be integrated into the journey, they can also be used as avoidance mechanisms. Remember that the focus of Ritual Practices is about more than optimization or "life hacking." It is always about coming more alive. And it's never about the practice itself either, as if it is some sort of spiritual hobby. The practices are about something much more important: getting your heart back.

Throughout the chapters of this book, I'll be sharing a number of Ritual Practices that I discovered and practiced over the course of my journey, such as solitude, dreamwork, wandering in the wild, meditation, and many more. My goal is not to do a deep dive into each practice, but to give you enough of a sense of the substance of each one so that you can continue your own exploration and experimentation—marked by humility and respect for lineage, context, and intent—as you cultivate your own ecosystem of practices.

Try them on (it will take some time and often, repetition).

Take what is helpful. Leave what is not.

Ultimately, you will develop and expand your own collection of tools.

To assist you in locating in these pages the transformative tools I discuss, I've included a list at the back of this book. Additionally, I've provided a glossary of terms before this chapter to acquaint you with the *Language of the Journey* as you read and a resource list at the end of the book to support you in deepening your understanding of all three of the foundational elements of the way home—Mythical Pattern, Mystical Presence, and Ritual Practice.

The Narrow Way

What an incredible time to be alive. Tools and techniques to support us in all facets of our life are more available to us than at any point in history. Specifically, access to the stories and practices of religious and cultural traditions has opened up in unprecedented ways. One minute you're reading a 2,500-year-old quote from a Chinese philosopher on Instagram, and the next you hear a superstar athlete reference a rabbi from two millennia ago, before you stop by your local yoga studio to perform some ancient movements (and not a few new ones that may or may not be helpful but have really catchy names).

Exposure to all this knowledge is filled with potential. The barriers of authority, belief, and even geography no longer exist, or at least they aren't as strong, and this open access to the wisdom of the ages creates a lot of opportunities for growth and transformation. However, the prevalence of this knowledge can also dilute its power by creating the illusion that there are shortcuts en route to maturing into a wholehearted human ready to serve and bless the world.

But there are no shortcuts. Though access and information

and awareness of the way are as wide as the world, in truth, the way is narrow. Though all are welcome to walk in it, many will abandon the path because it operates in the opposite way from what we've become conditioned to expect. There are three particular aspects to the way that sober up any potential traveler who feels entitled to an easy journey.

First, the way is slow in a world that demands a quick fix. My own journey through the ten steps outlined in this book took place over the course of six years. Numerous times I was convinced that I had completed the journey, only to discover that I was merely unlocking the next challenging task. I had to shed a layer of myself. And then another. And another . . .

Second, the way doesn't guarantee success—at least not the "success" promised by self-help strategies that improve your bank account, abs, or influence. Instead, this way disrupts your life as you know it. Travel on this way and you may notice your emotions all over the map, your friends disappearing, and your dollars dwindling. Nevertheless, the place of wholeness, healing, fulfillment—this is the common destination for all who surrender to soul, even as the particularities look different for each person. I wonder where the way will take you . . .

Third, the way involves suffering. There is no easy way home. In order to mature into who you are and why you're here, your "false self" must die. This might not sound all that bad up front. But (spoiler alert!) when you begin this journey, the "false self" that must die *doesn't feel very false.* It has been calling the shots for years and has convinced you that *it is indeed* who you really are. This self-deception is precisely why it is so agonizing and painful to shed layer after layer of this false identity to get to that core, essential you.

None of these qualities tend to be very desired. They don't get many clicks or sell very well, which is why, as one ancient sage said, "Small is the gate and narrow the road that leads to life, and only a few find it."

A Way for the World

Though the way is narrow, no matter how you are losing your heart or have already lost it, this way is waiting for you.

Indeed it is filled with challenges and threats and chaos and uncertainty. It is tempting to skip out or try to go through the motions. It is tempting to outsource the journey. But no one else can do it for you. No friend or spouse. No coach or therapist. No influencer or guru. The journey is yours alone.

But know this: *Those who seek will find. For those who knock, the door will be opened.*

To anyone who bravely decides to step out of the status quo and into this less-traveled way, nourishment will be provided, supportive angels will arrive, and an inner fortitude will be accessed along the way to the greatest reward—the reclamation of what poet Mary Oliver calls your "one wild and precious life," a life of meaning and belonging, wisdom and love.

In the beginning, you won't feel ready for the risk. You won't feel equipped for the disorienting quest. You won't be open to forfeiting everything you've constructed in order to claim the life you're meant to live. That's okay. This is to be expected at first. Then, little by little, you will become friends with the unknown.

Often you will feel alone, whether you are just setting out

or already far along on the treacherous trek. In many ways, this will be true because the journey is yours alone. This will be difficult. But as you continue, you will realize you are not alone. The stories in this book and people you encounter along the way will remind you that you are accompanied by a caravan of travelers. A *great cloud of witnesses*. Many who have gone before you. Others who are alongside you right now. Still more who have yet to begin their adventure.

Yes, you will lose so much. But what you will gain is incomparable. You will find the life that is truly yours. You will have a new readiness and clarity about how to make generative contributions to your community and to the world. And you will be counted among the true heroes, having invested your one life in the flourishing of others.

Getting your heart back . . . finding your way home.

Of course, this matters for you.

But it also matters *beyond you*.

For your community, for the world, for future generations.

Healing yourself heals the world. From anxiety and distraction, hostility and violence, greedy consumption and environmental degradation.

Waking yourself up wakes up the world. From deception and exploitation, cowardice and self-preservation.

When you get your heart back, your life becomes a song, inviting neighbors and strangers, young and old, to walk in the world in a new way, reclaiming a wider, wilder vision of what it means to be human and belong to one another.

So this is what the world needs now:

The world needs you to get your heart back.

Because if *you* don't have your heart, *we* have nothing . . .

PHASE ONE
Leaving the Familiar

was sitting around the table with my two daughters one afternoon, racing through emails while they were coloring and chatting, when, suddenly, an unannounced visitor arrived.

It was a hummingbird.

It snuck into the house through the front door, which had been left slightly ajar to let in the fresh spring air. It dashed around for a few moments. Then it landed on the windowsill where it remained motionless. Watching the stranded creature, my daughters squealed with delight while I anxiously wondered, *How did it find its way to our front door? Is it injured? How can we help?*

I opened the door wide, hoping the hummingbird would embrace its freedom to fly away. But it didn't. It needed our help. I was too afraid to touch it—maybe I would crush it or hurt its wings. However, my oldest daughter, nine years old at the time, was fearless. She crept up to the tiny creature and tried to grab it. Instantly, the bird buzzed its wings. My daughter nervously retracted her hand. She took a breath and then extended her hand again and again (while I dispensed my amateur hummingbird-handling advice from a distance).

After more than a dozen attempts, she tried something different. She caressed the bird's head. It relaxed. So she wrapped her tiny hands around the hummingbird, and this time it didn't resist. "Shhh," she whispered, carrying it to the front door. Then she let go. She set it free. The beautiful bird darted away from our house. Into the flowers and trees of our neighborhood. Back to its true home where it was always meant to be.

And so it is also for anyone who sets out on the journey of wholeness. The three steps of the Leaving phase mirror this hummingbird's adventure.

You find yourself in a place you don't fit or a situation that doesn't work anymore.

You need help—and likely resist it for a while.

Ultimately, you need to get out of whatever house you're in so you can find your true home.

My own inauguration into this Leaving the familiar phase happened on that rainy morning run when the inner voice interrupted me. I knew immediately that it was time for a change. What I *didn't* know was all that I had outgrown—social roles, emotional patterns, styles of relating, religious affiliations, and more. Nor did I realize that it would take years, and a whole bunch of starts and stops, to navigate my way through this first phase of the quest. And then, even still, I would have a long way to go before I was home.

"Concerning all acts of initiative or creation, there is one elementary truth . . . that the moment one definitely commits oneself, then Providence moves too. . . . A whole stream of events issues from the decision, raising in one's favor all manner of incidents and meetings and material assistance which no man would have believed would have come his way."

—W. H. Murray,
The Scottish Himalayan Expedition

"But whether small or great, and no matter what the stage or grade of life, the call rings up the curtain, always, on a mystery of transfiguration—a rite, or moment, of spiritual passage, which, when complete, amounts to a dying and a birth."

—Joseph Campbell,
The Hero with a Thousand Faces

1

ANSWER THE CALL

The Call to Adventure

The way home always begins with an invitation.

Life seems to be moving along just fine when all the sudden you receive a summons to another way. It comes in a multitude of forms. An offhand comment by a friend, a chance encounter with a stranger, or, like me, a voice from within.

Sometimes the invitation arrives in a single moment. It's a sudden crisis that comes in the form of a phone call, firing, diagnosis, or accident. A car crash shatters the hands of Marvel's Doctor Strange—and his successful career as a surgeon. A blinding light on the road to Damascus puts an end to the persecuting ways of the Bible's Saul of Tarsus, who later becomes St. Paul, the proclaimer of good news.

The invitation comes as a series of signs, too. You keep running into dead ends. Or your relationship continues to deteriorate. Or you notice a recurring theme in your life. Four times the gods approach the Buddha in disguise before he responds, leaves behind his privileged life, and steps into his calling.

This invitation is the Call to Adventure.

It is life's way of expelling us from the school of duties and obligations that have restricted us from growing and changing.

It is the sounding of an alarm, urging you to exit the outdated version of your life.

Whether it arrives in whispered warnings or the clashing sound of everything falling apart, this is how the way home begins.

Answering yes to this call is the first step.

Refusing the Call

Immediately after receiving my *If you don't have your heart, you have nothing* invitation, I stumbled home, crawled into bed in my rain-drenched clothes, and pulled the covers over my head.

I knew there was something generative and hopeful about what I had heard. But the words also opened my eyes to the fact that I was broken—I couldn't unsee this reality. I could sense the vague outline of the daunting task in front of me and it made me want to check out of all my responsibilities and hide forever in a dark hole. I wanted to quit everything.

I had just received a gift. And yet, I was on the brink of ignoring my Call to Adventure.

I realized later that I actually had been refusing the call for a long, long time.

There are a million ways to refuse the call.

You can escape to all sorts of things. Pills, porn, a promotion. A bigger bank account, bigger biceps, a better buzz. Romantic conquests on Tinder. A Tesla. A trip to Tahiti. New home improvement tools or the latest technological gadgets.

Or you can ignore the invitation by trying to double down on the illusion of safety, stability, and security. Tinker with your insurance policies or obsess even more about that retirement account. Micromanage your kids' activities and achievements. Cling to religious certainty.

You can even refuse the call by creating conflict in your relationships or workplace, blowing up your life so you can blame others and avoid the invitation to the inner journey.

The list goes on and on. And while some forms of avoidance might be more destructive than others, they are all designed to distract you from the wild adventure that is waiting for you.

Recognizing the Call

The refusal techniques are abundant. But the good news is that there are conditions that often precede the invitation: discontentment, transitions, and suffering. I didn't notice these conditions in my life, which is why I didn't recognize the call until that rainy morning interruption. Knowing these conditions prepares you to recognize the call instead of disappearing into distraction. They are signals, giving you the opportunity to align yourself with the flow of life rather than resisting until a major course correction is necessary.

First, discontentment with some aspect of your life—relationship status, career situation, financial picture, health condition, geographical location—can be a sign that you are being invited to migrate into what the famous Swiss psychiatrist and psychoanalyst Carl Jung referred to as *the second half of life*. I had been discontent for over a year. No longer in the exhilarating startup phase, my work had become both boring and overwhelming. Meanwhile, my marriage felt monotonous, and I was emotionally checked out. While it can be easy to fixate on whatever issue is frustrating you, discontentment is actually a cue to stay curious. Because it is often about the issue behind the issue. Your heart wants you to be more whole and is trying to be heard.

Second, life transitions also suggest a ripening for a Call to Adventure. *If you don't have your heart, you have nothing* happened to me when I was in the middle of a six-month transition out of my job as director of the community center I cofounded. The invitation often meets us when we are in the in-between spaces of life. Graduation. Marriage. Divorce. Parenthood. Retirement. In these times of transition, we are already breaking out of the confines of familiar routines and responsibilities. We are ready to face some degree of the unknown. Which is why the stirrings of the soul wisely see this as an opportunity to rise to the surface. Liminal spaces are a time to listen carefully.

Third, perhaps the most powerful condition for hearing a Call to Adventure is suffering. Suffering is another form of transition—often the unchosen transition. Suffering disrupts what once was. *Things will never be the same again.* It results from a moment or season of crisis. You get fired or your partner cheats on you. You tear your Achilles tendon playing basketball. You find out you can't have children. You receive a cancer diagnosis. A loved one dies, suddenly or after prolonged pain. A global pandemic alters life on a massive scale. Whatever incident causes the suffering either *is* the Call to Adventure or sets the stage for the call that is about to come.

Suffering comes in many forms, some more catastrophic than others. But it doesn't matter what the volume level of your suffering is because any suffering that is not acknowledged or grieved leads to more pain, and to bitterness, anger, and isolation. Pain that is not processed is passed on, remember. When we face our suffering, however, we can emerge more tender, open, and grateful for the gift of life—a condition that makes us more ready to find our way home.

My suffering came in the form of the burnout that stealthily was robbing me of energy, desire, and concern. It arose from the weight of responsibility and expectations that I burdened myself with. And it also arrived in experiencing the betrayal of close friends and colleagues. My announcement that I was transitioning out of the executive director role at the community center six months earlier had triggered something in the people who were intimately involved in the center's work. In their fear of change and anxiousness about how my transition would impact them (all very natural feelings!), they lashed out at me with anger, blame, and rejection. I had poured everything into that place and I had given them my all. Besides, I wasn't just jumping ship; I was transitioning carefully to ensure that the center would thrive even more after I was gone. Receiving the brunt of their reactions was painful and debilitating.

Just like the conditions of discontentment and transition, my suffering was an indication that my center of gravity was shifting. But I couldn't quite put the puzzle pieces together. That's why it ultimately took a mystical interruption to amplify my Call to Adventure and plunge me into the quest.

Saying Yes

The seed of my *Yes* response to the call was planted the day of that rainy morning run and whisper from within when I finally got out of bed later that morning. It grew when, thanks to my wife Cherie's urging, I decided to take the day off instead of hiding in my work. And my *Yes* began to bloom when I showed up at a previously scheduled lunch appointment with my mentor Ron.

I sat across the restaurant booth from him and spilled out my unsorted thoughts. "Everything is falling apart," I told him. He listened. He acknowledged my hurt and confusion. And he offered words of hope: "You are much more buoyant than you feel in this moment."

He was right.

I was struggling, but I hadn't drowned yet.

After lunch, we went for a stroll. He popped into a store and when he came out, he handed me a journal.

"Write it all down," he said.

So I did.

Over the next few days, the words poured out of me. Every word I wrote was a *Yes* to the invitation to get my heart back. Keeping a journal was not foreign to me, but over the years it had become all about plans, projects, and productivity. About going *forward*, not going *inward*. The journaling that began in that season was different, and it has been with me ever since: a space to chronicle my own unfolding personal myth, with all of its visions and confrontations, mysterious dreams and sacred encounters, rituals and poetry.

A journaling practice is a space to excavate your life story in search of your meaning and purpose.

A journaling practice is a space to listen to your life.

As the weeks went on, journaling unearthed more of my exhaustion and sadness. It was hard, but movement was happening in my life. And I wanted more of it. More signs. More guidance. Anything to prove that I wasn't making this whole thing up and that I was on the right track to finding my heart.

Of course, more signs would come. They always do. You just have to be willing to say *Yes*. And *Yes* again.

The Girl and the Jaguar Tattoo

I didn't want to miss any signs, so I picked up a book about how to listen for the voice of God. In other words, how to awaken your *awakened brain*. How to activate your mystical receptors. It encouraged curiosity about daily experiences, noticing patterns or recurring symbols you come across, and paying attention to the moments that catch you off guard.

So I remained vigilant.

And then one day . . . I saw a sign.

On a crowded bus, my two-and-a-half-year-old daughter pointed at a burly man behind us whose arms were covered in tattoos.

"Daddy, get a tattoo," she said.

I didn't even know she knew that word. It caught me off guard. So I paid attention.

"If you got a tattoo, what would you get?" I asked.

"A heart," she answered.

How sweet, I thought. *A little cliché, but sweet.*

"And what tattoo should daddy get?" I asked, thinking she would have a cute little idea for me too.

She wrinkled her forehead, hesitated, and declared:

"A jaguar. You should get a jaguar tattoo."

That came out of nowhere! *A jaguar?* I didn't think she knew what that was either. I thought about what the book said and tucked *jaguar* in the back of my mind, wondering if it might mean something for me. It didn't take long to find out.

While I was watching a college football game that afternoon, *jaguar* popped back into my mind. *Maybe it's a symbol,* I thought. My mind drifted to the remote Mayan village in Mexico where I spent a summer fifteen years earlier. I thought about the revered place of the jaguar in Mayan mythology and art. It felt like a huge stretch, but maybe it represented something to them then that it also represented for me now.

At the exact moment I was about to google "jaguar mayan symbol" on my phone, a commercial came on the TV. A sleek SUV was winding its way through rolling hills. Even though I'm not at all a car guy, I was mesmerized. I had never seen this vehicle before. I kept watching. As the commercial ended, the car company logo appeared on the screen. And there it was: a brand-new Jaguar automobile.

In an instant, with incredible dexterity, I redeployed my thumb and altered my search. I followed *jaguar* with the first word that entered my mind at that moment: *motto.* I clicked the search button. I scrolled down a couple search results and I gasped at the three words I saw: *Grace, Space, Pace.*

I would go on to click the link. I would read that this was

the Jaguar luxury car company's slogan in the 1950s and '60s. I would see that for those cars this slogan meant *elegant, roomy, fast*. But before any of this, I knew. I knew that these words were meant for me. *Grace, Space, Pace*. Not only did this trio of words add additional confirmation to the rainy morning invitation I had received. But they were also instructions, offering me three ways to say *Yes* to the call, three critical practices I needed to embrace if I wanted to discover my way home.

Grace, Space, Pace

So—let's hit the brakes for a second and get this straight—a man on the bus, a two-year-old's "jaguar tattoo" idea, a TV commercial, and a *Mad Men*–era car slogan all came together to provide guidance for my life?

That is correct.

Maybe it was all just a coincidence.

Maybe I was looking for meaning where none existed.

But what did I have to lose? What do *we* have to lose in these moments? Why not follow the signs, as ridiculous as they may seem, and see where they lead?

I chose to adopt these words—originally meant for a luxury car—for myself. I chose to receive them as a sacred gift. And it was worth it because this message altered the course of my life. It pointed me toward Ritual Practices that have been critical to my journey ever since.

Grace, Space, Pace.

These were not only three ways for *me* to say *Yes* to the call to get my heart back.

They are powerful for *anyone* who practices them.

They always have been.

Space: Finding Solitude

Space was the first one to get my attention.

It spoke to me immediately of Solitude.

Solitude is intentional aloneness. It is about making space to hear what the Quakers call the "still, small voice" within. To listen to your heart, to connect with God, to tune in to reality. As the lives of the great spiritual teachers demonstrate, solitude is a primary form of sustenance and guidance on the path of awakening. Siddhartha Gautama sat alone under the Bodhi tree for seven weeks and became the Buddha. Jesus went into the wilderness for forty days and forty nights to figure out his identity, and he regularly withdrew to the desert for time alone. Muhammad retreated to a cave where he received his first revelation and would later spend a month there each year. They all needed solitude. They all needed *Space*.

Luke Skywalker did too. He spent a chunk of time on the remote swamp planet Dagobah doing handstands, wielding the force, and learning from Yoda's confusing sentences. *Space* away from his Rebel Alliance community was a necessity in order to prepare for the next phase of his journey.

Henri Nouwen, a priest who left behind prestigious academic teaching to care for individuals with intellectual and developmental disabilities, writes in *The Way of the Heart* that solitude is "the furnace of transformation." Solitude is where you shed your false self—your Impostor—and come back to who you truly are.

And as activist and author bell hooks often said, solitude is "central to the art of loving." It fills us up to love ourselves and to love others. Which explains why my love for others was in short supply in the season leading up to my Call to Adventure. It had been ages since I took space for myself.

Many years earlier, I had a regular solitude practice. I would get off the grid every week at an old mansion overlooking Puget Sound that had been converted into a retreat center run by Dominican nuns. Sister Judy always welcomed me. Then I would pray and walk around, read and write. Sometimes I would fall asleep. That was okay, too. Every time I left, I felt renewed.

But then our three children arrived, one after the other. The startup organizations grew from ideas to living, breathing things. And there were people everywhere. Neighbors trapped in trauma who needed care. Staff and community members creating and coordinating who needed my support. Friends celebrating or suffering who needed my presence. And always, somewhere, a baby of mine who needed a diaper change.

So I forgot about solitude for years.

Which meant I forgot about my heart too.

Until *Space* called out to me and told me I needed to court my heart again, a process that would require patience and practice.

After all, soul needs space. It gets scared away when life is stuffed to the brim with commitments and demands. Solitude cultivates that necessary space. The question is: how do you create space for solitude when your life is jam-packed?

The first thing that finding solitude often requires is *subtraction*.

If, like I was, you are overcommitted professionally, socially, or otherwise, then you need to create boundaries. You need to start saying "No." I stopped jumping in to do things that were the responsibility of others, stayed out of my email inbox, and spread out my meeting schedule. I also confronted my massive fear of missing out socially by no longer showing up for every single community activity and get-together with friends.

Sometimes it can be a hobby that is the culprit of consuming all your *Space*. When this is the case, then you probably need to start eliminating, or at least reducing, these activities because they might be distracting you from your inner world. What about those long rounds of golf or multiple fantasy football teams or endless home improvement projects? Interrogate yourself: is the activity stirring or squelching the soul?

Or perhaps you need to subtract possessions to find *Space*. Things don't just take up *physical* space. They take up *spiritual* space. That's why Jesus told a rich young man that he needed to sell everything to gain his true life and why the Buddha before him—a rich young man himself—renounced the wealth and status of his family to pursue enlightenment. These wisdom teachers knew that being preoccupied with buying, managing, organizing, and fixing your possessions can end up *possessing you*, distracting you from the one beautiful and daring life that is yours to live. Something as simple as a thrift shop drop-off, Craigslist sale, or writing a big check just might be the thing you need to create space.

In the process of finding solitude, after subtraction comes addition. Adding a solitude practice to your life comes in many forms: journaling, meditating, walking in nature, and many other practices that we will explore throughout this book.

For me, it began with yoga. More specifically, it began with me flailing around on a yoga mat in ratty basketball shorts and an old T-shirt while surrounded by Lululemon-wearing experts. But it didn't take long for my body and mind to relax. I was encountering a spaciousness I hadn't experienced in years. People were in the room with me, but I had found solitude.

Soon I was hooked. I subtracted working through lunch and added yoga in that time slot. Four or five times a week I would head to the studio, stretch, and sweat. The yoga was exhilarating, and so was the radical act of making space for myself in the middle of the day instead of losing myself in the demands and expectations of others.

As I sunk into the solitude that yoga provided, I had a painful but powerful realization: I was obsessed with performing for others. In my constant concern about what others were thinking about my sloppy yoga moves and disheveled attire, I could see more clearly that this was how I operated across my life. I was always worrying about what people thought of me, what they needed me to be, what role I should play. Imperfectly following the poses of the yoga teacher began to break me free from these carefully choreographed ways that I moved through the world. Feeling the movements of my body opened pathways to begin to feel the faint stirrings of my soul. My concerns about others faded away and I found a beautiful aloneness, the beginnings of being at home in myself.

Solitude was doing its slow, healing work on me.

That's what solitude does.

Pace: Practicing Sabbath

While the invitation to *Space* was consistent with the car motto's message of roominess, *Pace* communicated to me the opposite of what it meant for the luxury Jaguar. I didn't need to go faster; I needed to slow down.

It was a practice from my past that would reintroduce me to the art of slowing down: Shabbat.

Shabbat, or Sabbath as the Christian tradition I grew up in calls it, shows up in the opening scene of the Hebrew Bible. After six days of creating all the things, Elohim (one of the many names the Bible uses for God) rests on the seventh day.

Shabbat is the word used here for resting.

Clocking out.

Stopping.

Shabbat shows up again in the Ten Commandments. Because God rested on the seventh day, it says, humans should chill out too. No work. No busy activity. Just being. Being with God. Being with beloved community.

The idea evolved from there. Jewish communities developed detailed Shabbat practices from Friday sundown to Saturday sundown. Later Christians moved their Sabbath day of rest to Sunday. And now Chick-fil-A is closed on Sundays. In both traditions, Shabbat or Sabbath rest often involves a combination of religious ceremonies, restricted activities, communal meals, and perhaps the highly venerated afternoon nap (or, at least, telling your kids that's what you're doing).

I grew up with the Sabbath day. It meant church in the morning followed by a quiet day of *not* hanging out with friends, *not* playing organized sports, and *not* going to the mall (where else did a teen want to hang out in the nineties?). Fortunately, we could watch the Green Bay Packers, which my dad never got to enjoy on his stricter childhood Sundays. But still, my pace that day was set at a slower speed than my friends. It felt legalistic, and it was annoying.

Later, however, I started to appreciate a slower, sleepier Sunday pace to close out the weekend. But almost immediately I lost the option. As a pastor, Sunday became my busiest workday. I tried to integrate the spirit of Sabbath into my weekend beyond Sunday, but I could never figure it out—until about a decade in when I burned out and I had to. *Pace* was giving me a chance to reclaim this ancient practice for myself.

Shabbat is actually a radical idea. Christian theologian Walter Brueggemann calls the practice of sabbath a form of resistance. Tricia Hersey, an activist known as "the Nap Bishop," concurs when she says, "Rest is resistance." Against all of the powers and pressures that insist we are what we do, that reduce us to producers and consumers, that make everything a competition to do more and do it better, the Hebrew creation myth introduces the God-who-naps—and if God naps, then the people must do the same! Shabbat is an invitation into non-anxious, refreshing rest.

Pace urged me to give sabbath another try. This time not as an obligation, but as an opportunity. The magic of sabbath is that not only can it be applied to slowing down one day of the week, as in the traditional sense, but it can also be practiced in other creative and adaptive ways.

I started to notice ordinary sabbath practices all over the place. The way my children paused to huddle around a banana slug on an afternoon hike. My neighbor strolling down the block with his pet beagle. The stranger at the park on a blanket in the distance, reading a book.

I was inspired to change my *Pace*. So I declined meetings. I pressed pause on any new endeavors. I started practicing a version of "tech shabbat," a term I would become acquainted with a few years later. This involved resting from technology with simple practices like limiting my time online and putting my phone in the other room. I could feel it freeing me from the chains of *more, faster, now.*

Slowing down was a teacher. Just like solitude. This time, however, the lesson's emphasis was on my allegiance to producing and achieving. I began to see that my desire to succeed in my work wasn't just because of an urgent, compassionate desire to help our neighbors get clean, escape street-based sex work, put a roof over their head, and ultimately experience love and belonging. No. My motives were mixed, and not entirely selfless. There was a wounded part of me that was in it for the success, the victory, the attention. A part of me that believed that I am only loved for what I do and what I achieve. I was helping people, yes, but I was also chasing after acceptance. Changing my *Pace* was only the beginning of tracing my harmful beliefs about needing to earn love back through my life, family, and beyond. But it was a game-changer.

Grace: The Power of Pilgrimage

Ever since that morning run I felt like I was encountering a fresh Grace. A nourishing, healing energy and presence. But it wasn't until the following summer that I experienced a Ritual Practice that got through to me about Grace.

Nine months after my *If you don't have your heart you have nothing* moment, I received another form of Shabbat: a four-month sabbatical. While this extended break from work for rest and rejuvenation exists in academia and, increasingly, in some corporate settings, sabbatical is still a rare gift. I was fortunate enough to get one because it is not uncommon for pastors to receive a sabbatical after seven years. I was more than eight years into my work and eagerly welcomed the job perk.

Since work was so intertwined with every aspect of our life, we knew we had to get out of town. Cherie and I cleaned up the house, rented it out to help cover the cost of our adventures, and hit the road in our minivan with our seven-, six-, and three-year-olds. As soon as we left Seattle and drove over the Cascade Mountains, I felt a lightness I had not known for years. I felt gratitude for the adventure that was unfolding. I was also scared. I knew I needed this extended time to separate myself from the things solitude and shabbat had shown me—my pursuit of the approval of others and my belief that my worth is tied up in what I do and accomplish. But I also knew that I would have to face restless parts of myself, parts addicted to activity and afraid of fading into irrelevance.

The choice to leave our home for sabbatical was about more than just a change of scenery.

We were embarking on a pilgrimage.

A pilgrimage is an intentional journey to a place in which a person searches for the meaning of their life or for greater connection with self, God, others, and/or nature before returning back home. The outward physical journey is symbolic of the inner adventure that the traveler experiences during and beyond the pilgrimage.

The destination for a pilgrimage is often a shrine or place of importance in the religious tradition—the site of the temple or spiritual leader's birth or death or resurrection. In Islam, adult Muslims are required to take a *hajj* to Mecca, the birthplace of Muhammad, at some point during their lifetime. The Holy Land draws pilgrims from Christianity, Judaism, and Islam. Roman Catholics visit the Vatican. The Ganges River is the destination in the fifty-five-day Hindu *Kumbh Mela* pilgrimage. In Latin America, pilgrims travel to places the Virgin Mary has appeared. Meanwhile, Buddhist pilgrimage sites include multiple places from the Buddha's life. And Chaucer's fourteenth-century *Canterbury Tales* tells the story of a motley crew of thirty pilgrims leaving London to travel to the shrine of some guy named Thomas Becket in Canterbury (Look him up, I'm sure he was important).

But pilgrimages aren't just reserved for self-professed religious folks. In college, I walked a portion of the Camino de Santiago, an ancient network of pilgrimage trails that leads to the supposed remains of James, one of Jesus' closest followers, in the Spanish city of Santiago de Compostela. In recent years, the Camino has become hugely popular. Rather than participate for religious reasons, however, most pilgrims travel for recreational purposes or with their own spiritual intention.

Pilgrimages don't have to be to the places that religions identify as holy, either. Our travels took us to the homes of loved ones around the United States and Canada, to stunning natural places like the Grand Canyon in Arizona and the Badlands in South Dakota, as well as the southern coast of Spain, a country dear to my heart. You can make your own pilgrimage to any place that is significant to you or that you're intrigued by. It could be the homeland of your ancestors, where you got engaged, or even—as is the case for so many people—Disney World. Ultimately, both the process and destination of a pilgrimage are made sacred by bringing your own intention to the journey.

One of the main intentions of our sabbatical pilgrimage was to *receive hospitality*, which is what pilgrimages depend on. After almost a decade of leading, guiding, facilitating, initiating, gathering, and convening, we knew it was time to be the guest, not the host. To get in touch with our needs, rather than just being needed by others. Like pilgrims, away from the familiarity and comforts of home, we relied on the people and places we visited. We were vulnerable in new ways.

During my Camino pilgrimage experience in college, hospitality came in the form of a loaf of bread, free pints in a pub, or the last bed in a hostel. Hospitality showed up again this time, now in midlife and with my whole family. After long days of gas station stops, tantrums, and family sing-alongs on the road, our friends would greet us with a delicious meal, a cold beverage, and a prepared place to sleep. Around evening fires and over morning coffee, they would inquire, *How are you, really?* Later, in Spain, strangers took care of us. Late-night snacks from an Airbnb host after an exhausting day of transatlantic travel. A farewell meal from the waitress at the corner cafe we visited each day.

It sounds ordinary, hospitality.

It is.

But if you pay attention, it also has this shimmering quality to it.

Because hospitality is always a fundamental lesson in Grace.

On this sabbatical pilgrimage, I started to receive this lesson deep in my bones. I wasn't in control. I wasn't in charge. I didn't need to have it all together. And that was okay. I was still loved. I belonged. I was a welcome guest.

For years, as a pastor, I had been talking about grace, this radical belief that all humans are worthy of love and compassion and care. It was the foundation of all my work, the energy that kept the community center running. "Come as you are," we said to our neighbors. But pilgrimage showed me that I didn't really get it. That I had a hard time receiving the help of others. That I was ruthless to myself, constantly pushing myself to do more and to get things perfectly right (whatever that means!). In reality, I was a stranger to grace.

This is the power of pilgrimage. It displays your vulnerability. It exposes your needs. It dismantles your sense of self-sufficiency. It exposes the illusion of control that is the root of perfectionism. And, ultimately, it helps you get a glimpse of your real self.

A New Beginning

I returned to Seattle from sabbatical a year after a ridiculous message brought to me by a toddler's tattoo idea and a TV commercial. Practicing the wisdom of *Grace, Space, Pace* changed me. I didn't have my heart back. I wasn't home yet. But I was on my way.

Throughout my sabbatical, whether I was relaxing on the

sparkling shores of the Mediterranean or driving across an empty stretch of Nebraska highway, amid all of the questions that had been swirling about life, work, home, family, and finances, one thing became clear: I had already transitioned out of the community center, but I now knew it was also time to leave my role as pastor of the neighborhood church I had started. In other words, I had to leave behind the other project and role that I had invested so much in, that I had defined myself by for almost a decade. Because *Grace, Space, Pace* had revealed to me that the only way I could continue my quest home—the only way I could grow up as a human being—was by separating myself from the roles and achievements that I had become so attached to.

This is how it always is on the way. Saying *Yes* to the invitation demands a departure from the familiar. My *Yes* began when I summoned the strength to get out of bed on that rainy morning. It continued with my embrace of the fresh patterns of solitude, sabbath, and pilgrimage that *Grace, Space, Pace* brought me. But my *Yes* started to get really real when I said goodbye to my job.

It was significant. Yet all of this was only just the beginning. Saying *Yes* to the invitation to get your heart back is only the start of the journey. Whether it is marked by external changes, such as a job change or cross-country move, or by invisible inner shifts, your *Yes* is never an arrival. In fact, it isn't even a full departure.

It's buying your plane ticket, but not yet getting on the plane.

It is step one of Leaving.

The beginning of the beginning.

As I stepped out into the beginning of the beginning, Irish poet John O'Donohue's blessing, "For a New Beginning," gave me comfort. It reminded me that I had been waiting for a fresh start for a while, that I could trust the call I had received, and that it was time to open up fully to the grace of this moment.

I liked how that sounded.

And that's exactly what I did.

I unfurled myself like a sail in the wind and began my voyage across the unknown sea.

"When you want something, all the universe
conspires in helping you to achieve it."

—**Paulo Coelho,**
The Alchemist

"One has only to know and trust, and
the ageless guardians will appear.
Having responded to his own call, and
continuing to follow courageously as the
consequences unfold, the hero finds all the
forces of the unconscious at his side."

—**Joseph Campbell,**
The Hero with a Thousand Faces

2

GET HELP

A Guide and a Gift

You alone must choose whether to embark on this journey. No one else can make the choice for you. No one else can do the inner work that is yours to do. This is true. But it's also true that you cannot travel home alone. To progress on the journey, you need the one thing every traveler needs: *Help*.

The good news is that a *Yes* to the call is always followed by help. A wise guide shows up—in the form of a person, a figure in a dream, a wild creature, or some other mystical way—and gives a gift to light the path, fend off foes, and beckon the traveler onward. An illumined teacher, say the *Upanishads*, is always there for the one who seeks self-realization.

Athena, the goddess of wisdom and war, assists Odysseus. She gives him a disguise and unbeatable strength so he can regain his throne.

Aaron helps his brother Moses, who "speaks with faltering lips," by delivering God's "Let my people go!" message to Pharaoh.

Obi-Wan Kenobi gives Luke Skywalker the lightsaber and becomes his Jedi Master.

The list goes on.

My initial guidance arrived immediately after my *If you don't have your heart you have nothing* invitation at my lunch meeting with Ron. He was the wizard in the woods, and the journal he gifted me was a magical charm to protect and direct me. That initial support sent me into the season of *Grace, Space, Pace,* and empowered me to shed the role that defined me for almost a decade. His help led to a new beginning.

But, as noted, it was still just the beginning of the beginning. A long, extended season of leaving life as I knew it. I had a lot more work to do. More parts of me to uncover, to confront, to heal. And to do this work in order to get my heart back, I needed more help.

Fortunately, as the Mythical Pattern demonstrates, help always arrives. Soon after you step through the portal by answering *Yes* to the call, support shows up. Long-dormant forces awaken and arrange themselves along your path in response to your *Yes*. You also start to notice for the first time the assistance that has always been around you. Whether you go looking for it or it comes to you—for anyone who says *Yes*, help always arrives right on time.

Getting help is unavoidable for anyone who wants to retrieve their heart. Because help plays a critical role in the essential work of identifying and shedding the false self.

Mascot Rules

Once upon a time I was a mascot for an arena football team. Not the gameday, halftime tricks mascot blasting a T-shirt gun. No, I was just the "community events" mascot. The one they sent to elementary school events, parades, and strange carnivals. I was a friendly but fierce rhinoceros named Blitz.

My first day on the job I sat around a small conference room table with the two other college students with whom I would share the musty, wearable-rug rhino costume as the staff intern instructed us:

There are two rules mascots must follow at all times:

First, do not talk. You can wave, point, blow a kiss, put one hand in front of your mouth and the other over your belly to imitate laughter, and make other gestures, but you cannot talk.

Second, do not take your mask off. Never, under any circumstances, let people see your face by removing your mascot head.

Our mascot task was to transport people to another world where, apparently, soft, fluffy rhinos roam free—to suspend reality for a moment (and build the team brand). A human voice or face would ruin that. These rules made sense in a mascot world. So whether I was hanging around creepy clowns, getting kicked in the shins by second graders, or dealing with women twice my age grabbing my butt (not a part of the costume, but my actual butt), I followed these rules.

But many years later, on this quest to get my heart back, I remembered the mascot rules.

And I realized they were essentially the same rules that I

obeyed in the non-mascot world—rules that were causing me to lose my heart!

Don't speak with your inner voice.

Don't let people see your true face.

We all follow these rules at one point or another. We all wear masks to keep the true self hidden. And following these rules in the real world has devastating consequences. It's how you lose your heart.

But getting *Help* helps you break these rules.

The Mask Task

Carl Jung uses the word *persona* to describe the masks we wear to conceal our true nature. Persona is how we present ourselves to others, the surface version of ourselves that we display for others in a moment, or indefinitely. It is an externalized, distorted version of ourselves put forward by our inner ego, which is who we think ourselves to be.

Personas are learned early in life. Adopting a persona is a strategy for survival and self-protection. It helps us to avoid the pain of being an outcast on the playground. It works to ensure that we are accepted instead of rejected by our families. In more extreme cases, it seeks to shield us from the rage and violence around us. Persona keeps us safe.

Until it doesn't anymore.

Eventually, as helpful and loyal as a persona has been, it no longer serves us. Building and maintaining the persona becomes a hindrance that keeps us ignoring our inner world. When we continue to wear a mask long past its expiration date, concealing that which is most real about ourselves, it turns into an adversary. Friend becomes foe. Persona no longer is a protector; it's an impostor. A phony. A false self. And when we let the Impostor run the show, our real life begins to slip away.

Soul begins to shrink.

It sneaks out the back door.

Like it did for me.

But it doesn't have to be this way. We can shed the mask we have been wearing—class clown, tough guy, victim, nice person, helper, achiever, or whatever our particular mascot costume is—and grow up into our fullest self. In fact, this is the fundamental task of the Leaving phase.

This is where *Help* comes in. You might sense that there is a deeper, truer you, but you need support to discover it. Because the longer you wear the mask, the more convinced you are that this Impostor actually *is* who you are, and the more you try to cling to it. You also need *Help* because the people closest to you may also resist your molting process, which adds immense social pressure to keep wearing the mask long after it has served its original purpose.

When *Help* arrives, it is like a mirror. It keeps us aware of the masks we wear. It reminds us of the true face behind the self-limiting faces we've presented to the world. It confronts our illusions. It calls out how we're fooling ourselves. *Help* is needed to recognize the mask (or masks!). To admit the mask exists. To identify the role it plays. To begin to peel off the mask. And to sustain the long, slow, and excruciating removal process.

Resistance to Assistance

The problem, however, is that even as we start to realize that we need help with our masks, we experience a resistance to assistance. The resistance is both internal and external.

The first barrier for many of us, especially men, is that we are taught from a young age to be strong, tough, and self-sufficient. As a result, we bury any sadness or struggle. We keep our feelings and our problems to ourselves. We hide from our partners, friends, and the people closest to us. Even as there has been a growing awareness and support around mental health in recent years, many people are still heavily resistant to getting support. We come up with excuses:

I'm a very private person.

I don't want anyone getting into my business.

I'm too busy for that sort of thing.

But if we're really honest, we're afraid of what we might discover when we look inside.

Even though society promotes self-sufficiency and obsesses over the success stories of supposedly self-made individuals, like the guy who started the company in his garage or the superstar athlete, the truth is that even heroes get *Help*. Finding your way home has always and forever involved *Help*. The illusion of independence is actually one of the masks that needs to be named and shed. Only then is a traveler ready to receive the help that is waiting in the wings.

The second problem with getting help is that we have become disconnected from the delivery systems for support. Cultural and religious traditions have long practiced elaborate systems of initiation into new phases of life, such as aboriginal rites of passage, bar and bat mitzvahs in Judaism, and confirmation in the church, which typically included instruction from guides and elders who were further down the road. *Help* was built into the journey of growing up. But now, detached from these traditions, many people are lacking these support systems and the helpful accompaniment that came with them.

The third form of resistance we might face is that good *Help* can be hard to find! In our immature Western culture there is dramatic shortage of "initiated" adults—people who have shed the false self and gone on the hero's journey. Just because a person is *older* doesn't make them an *elder*. True elders are well versed in the journey of Leaving the familiar, Falling into the unknown, and Rising to wholeness. They carry deep wisdom and know how and when to dispense it.

Nevertheless, while getting *Help* may be difficult, it is absolutely possible—and essential!

We just need to know where to look.

Anam Cara

The Celtic Christian tradition has a term that captures the kind of *Help* we need to be set free from the Impostor versions of ourselves: *anam cara*. It means "soul friend." A person who is a close companion on the spiritual journey. The term initially referred to a teacher, companion, or spiritual guide in the Celtic church. An *anam cara* is someone with whom you can share the most tender and truest parts of yourself. With no mask. No pretense. Just real and raw. An *anam cara* helps you ask: *What is this mask*

I've been wearing? Why? What am I hiding? Who is that behind the mask? Who am I really? It reflects back to you the personas you are shedding and the person you are becoming—so you can see who you truly are.

Frodo had such a companion in the loyal and courageous Samwise Gamgee in the *Lord of the Rings* trilogy. Rumi, Sufi Muslim mystic and poet, had his beloved friend and muse, Shams. For John of the Cross, the sixteenth-century Spanish Catholic mystic and author of *The Dark Night of the Soul,* it was the influential theologian and Carmelite nun Teresa of Avila who was his *anam cara*.

The Buddhist tradition has a similar concept. The term *kalyana mitra* describes a spiritual friend—literally, in Sanskrit, a "good kindness." This is not just a drinking buddy or golf buddy or cycling buddy, though it may be that too. This is someone who demonstrates a fierce and loyal kindness to you, drawing out the truest and highest version of yourself.

There are many different incarnations of *anam cara* or *kalyana mitra*. Trusted friend. Neighbor. Lover. Or a more formal role, like an AA sponsor or a paid professional such as therapist or spiritual director. It also can come in a communal form, like a spiritual congregation or small group, a band of brothers or a sisterhood. And just like the initial invitation, the *anam cara* kind of help can even come in a moment, through an unanticipated conversation with a stranger or chance encounter with an old acquaintance.

Whatever form it takes, *anam cara* holds a safe and brave space that separates what is false from what is true about who you are. To be clear, this process doesn't just soothe and calm;

it also disrupts and disturbs. To apply an often-repeated axiom, the role of the *anam cara* is to comfort the afflicted and afflict the comfortable. A true guide does not enable you to bypass pain and suffering. They don't let you ignore your shadow—the patterns of thought, feeling, and action that you don't want to be true about you. Instead, through their loving presence, an *anam cara* equips you to face your pain and see your shadow, even if it hurts to do so. Because wholeness is on the other side of that crucial work.

On my way home, I experienced the power of *anam cara* in three ways: friendship, spiritual direction, and wisdom teachers.

My Soul Friend

A few months after my sabbatical, as the new year began, I experienced a surge of creativity that I hadn't felt in ages. So within a few weeks of leaving my old job, I did what countless white guys in midlife do: I started a podcast. I also launched a nonprofit consulting practice. Both endeavors focused on themes I deeply cared about: spirituality, community, and social change. But this was a new chapter. I was now focused on supporting others who were doing the grassroots work that I had been involved in for over a decade.

I was in a good place. Thrilled about the external changes in my life, the fresh work and rhythms. Grateful for the internal shifts that had led to it—new discoveries, greater awareness, deeper presence. Satisfied from enduring the journey of the previous eighteen months. I felt like I had figured something out, like I had *completed* something. Life felt spacious and the future felt wide open and full of possibility. At least, it did for a couple of months.

As the novelty wore off, I realized there were a whole bunch of unpleasant feelings lurking in the shadows that I was ignoring—fear, sadness, jealousy, and confusion. I definitely had begun to identify my Impostor during my sabbatical pilgrimage, but I was still aggressively clinging to my masks. I needed help to face these feelings. I needed an *anam cara*.

During the long season of transition, I received love and care from a handful of close friends. Acquaintances encouraged me too, like when a guy I barely knew saw right through me and said, "Dude, take the pressure off of yourself of being awesome." And, of course, Cherie was a rock-solid support, even as she was undergoing her own process of morphing and evolving. She regularly reminded me, "You are not what you do." I needed to hear it every time.

But it was especially a character from my past who became my soul friend in this season: my best friend, Nico. A man with kind eyes and a legendary laugh. A devoted, mischievous, and huge-hearted human being. Simultaneously able to talk about the most profound spiritual things and the most outrageous things. We had become friends fifteen years earlier during a college semester in Spain. Nico and I shared a deep bond because of a mystical experience we shared on a park bench in Seville, our similar passionate approaches to life, and the fact that we had traveled down similar vocational paths.

We always joked that Nico copied whatever I did. I grew my hair out, so did he. I drove a Hyundai Elantra, then he got one. After four years of dating, I married Cherie. He dated Julie for only three months, but booked a wedding for just a few weeks after ours. Now, just as I was becoming increasingly lost in my mid-thirties, he was in the midst of his own midlife struggle. Go figure.

When my business of coaching and consulting leaders of faith-based communities, organizations, and churches stalled after about a year, I was offered a job doing similar work with a larger organization. It was part of the church denomination that I grew up in. It no longer fit me spiritually—which would become more and more apparent as time went on—but my intention would be to operate as a sort of undercover agent who encouraged the best parts of the system and functioned as a kind of sandpaper (and sometimes a buzz saw!) to the worst parts of it. It had all sorts of issues, but *I can change the system from the inside,* I thought.

And so, somewhat reluctantly, I took the job. The best part, however, was that it allowed me to cross paths with Nico again after a decade of rarely seeing each other while we lived more than a thousand miles apart and were busy raising families (It also eventually brought me to Berlin, where I went to a karaoke bar that featured a small, underground David Hasselhoff museum, but that's a story for another time).

Every couple of months Nico and I got to hang out on work trips. During morning workouts, in conference hallways, or over late-night gin and tonics, we would talk. And talk and talk. Mystical stories and spiritual practices, struggles and fears, and lots and lots of questions:

How do I know I'm on the right path?
What if I'm getting this all wrong?

How long do I wait for more clarity before making a decision?
What if I fail my family?
What if I fall flat on my face?
What am I doing with my life?

Our friendship embodied what the mystic Teresa of Avila once wrote in a letter about her relationship with John of the Cross: "What a wonderful thing it is for two souls to understand each other, for they neither lack something to say, nor grow tired." And it was an expression of an ancient proverb: "As iron sharpens iron, so one person sharpens another." (Not that I know anything about iron.)

Just as the hobbit Sam couldn't carry the ring to Mount Doom, but he could carry Frodo, Nico couldn't face my fears for me. He couldn't shed my masks for me. But he carried me. He held up a mirror so I could see all the old patterns I was repeating; my pretending, producing, and perfecting. In the "good kindness" of his presence, I was reminded I didn't have to follow the mascot rules. I could show my face. I could use my voice. I could just be myself.

Spiritual Companionship

Many people, especially men, report being lonely and not having a close friend they can be vulnerable with. (Remember that whole "pressure to be strong, tough, and self-sufficient" thing?) If this is you, that's okay. There are two pieces of good news for you.

First, when you answer *Yes* to the call, your desire to venture beneath the surface of casual conversation will increase. Because you *feel* more vulnerable, you will want to *be* more vulnerable with others. You will develop a sixth sense for meaningful connection, both drawing new friends to you and noticing the supportive communities that may already exist around you. Follow those leads and you may find a friend for life, or at least receive a gift of guidance for the moment you are in.

Second, remember that there are many versions of *anam cara*. One of the powerful alternative expressions of *Help* is a spiritual director.

Spiritual direction, also known as spiritual companionship, is an ancient form of accompaniment marked by compassionate presence and deep listening. It aims to help a person grow in self-knowledge, exercise discernment, and deepen mystical experience. A spiritual director holds space for you to explore your story and brings wisdom from their own spiritual experience.

In other words, a spiritual director is a professional who is trained and experienced in the art of being a *soul friend*.

I started to see a spiritual director a year and a half after leaving my job—three full years after my Call to Adventure! Any excitement I had about the changes in my professional life had worn off. I was increasingly confused. Even bitter. And a heavy sadness was following me around that I didn't understand. Something felt stuck inside me, and no amount of deep journaling or clumsy yoga or even friendship was able to release it. I needed more help.

While I was exploring therapist options, a friend raved to me about his own experience with spiritual direction. I was intrigued, so he gave me his spiritual director's email address. Soon I met Tim. He was really tall, with a kind face and curious eyes, and a hat that reminded me of Indiana Jones. I immediately sensed the spaciousness and strength of his presence.

Once a month Tall Tim and I would sit on a park bench, go for a walk, or meet in a coffee shop, and I would process what I was going through. I didn't have to filter anything with him. In his mirroring presence, my shadow—the parts of myself that I rejected and refused to acknowledge because they were negative or wrong or bad—slowly became visible. I felt safe to name the shadowy things I didn't want to face:

I regret my career choice and wish I had chosen something where I made more money. How foolish!

I'm jealous of friends who are achieving things in their work. Why not me?

I don't feel like I'm qualified to do anything anymore. What am I even good at?

I'm embarrassed to be working in this religious institution. I don't believe any of this stuff anymore. How could I still be here?

My capacity to love is in short supply. Have I ever really loved without an agenda?

These kinds of confessions, surfaced through spiritual direction, acquainted me with the insecurities, fears, and negative energies on the undersides of the masks I wore. I could see the kind of person I would have become if I had never had the space with Tall Tim to name these things: bitter, angry, lazy, judgmental, stingy.

In my time with Tall Tim, I also realized how sad I was. I grieved that a beautiful season of life was over. I wept over how my friends had treated me as I transitioned out of the work I loved. I was even sad *about bottling up my sadness* over the years and just pushing forward, and about what that had cost me and those around me.

There was also another, more complicated type of sadness that spiritual direction revealed. It was a selfish kind of sadness, the sadness of having to move on from my inner Impostor. It is the *false self* that is sad and humbled, observes Franciscan priest Richard Rohr in *Falling Upward,* because its game is over. I carried this kind of selfish sadness because leaving my old ways meant that I could no longer depend on the persona that used to make things happen for me, and its ambition and drive and lust for more. I had to move on from the version of myself that (I thought) people knew and loved. That way of being in the world was all I knew. Who would I be without it? And what would I do?

I wasn't sure. But I knew that sitting with and sifting through this devastating feeling was going to take more time, and that it was all a part of me getting my heart back. And I knew that Tall Tim was right there beside me, like a guardian angel. Like a biblical angel, which literally means *messenger,* Tall Tim was a messenger to me of new life and freedom and possibility. The message that his presence whispered to me was the same one that the angels of the Bible often delivered: *Do not be afraid.*

Wisdom Teachers

The seven-hundred-verse *Bhagavad Gita,* the sacred Hindu scripture, opens on the eve of a great war—an allegory for the inner battle that each human faces to find fulfillment. Prince

Arjuna is overwhelmed by the fight in front of him. He turns to his charioteer Krishna for guidance. Krishna (who also happens to be the god Vishnu) gives Prince Arjuna the gift of yoga lessons to sustain him. Not yoga *asanas,* or poses like the ones I sweated through that the western world often thinks about, but practical knowledge about how to discipline the mind so that one may experience union with the divine and be more fully human in the world.

The third kind of *Help* I received was more like the kind of support that Prince Arjuna received. Or like Jesus' disciples. Less talking, more listening. I found myself surrounded by a community of wise teachers who articulated truths about the world from their experience. All because of the podcast I started. My task was to ask the questions.

Initially, I launched the project to share stories and practical tips for leaders doing community organizing, spiritual formation, and innovative expressions of faith. But in light of a wave of events transpiring around the country, the podcast quickly became an avenue for me to dig even deeper and investigate racism, the treatment of women and LGBTQ+ people, and other systemic injustices. Most of my guests were people with different identities than my own. Not white, straight men who were so often the people that had been my teachers. I needed to learn from other voices, other experiences.

Just like my friendship with Nico and my spiritual direction with Tall Tim, these potent conversations held up a mirror to expose the illusions under which I was living. It became clear to me that my commitment to performing, producing, and perfecting wasn't just a personal problem. And it wasn't just the result of the family system I was born into and grew up in. It was a much bigger issue stemming from ideas of white superiority and a malformed masculinity.

In various ways, the wisdom teachers on my podcast repeatedly named what I later read in Yale Divinity School professor Willie James Jennings's book, *After Whiteness: An Education in Belonging,* where he identifies the agenda at the root of Western education. The goal, he says, is to create a self-sufficient man who embodies what he calls, ironically, three *virtues*: possession, control, and mastery. It is an individualistic, antagonistic approach to the human experience, committed to conquest and domination. It rejects wholeness and belonging. It denies humility, vulnerability, and curiosity.

The *Possession-Control-Mastery* orientation to life, embraced and perpetuated by white descendants of Europeans, was behind the brutal enslavement of Africans and their American-born descendants for nearly three centuries, and all the oppressive laws that followed. It was behind the systematic genocide of Native Americans and their forced removal from their lands. And it is behind the pillaging of the earth's natural resources for profit. The *Possession-Control-Mastery* trio has shown up in different cultures across time and place—and continues to—wherever there is the hoarding of power, the reduction of human beings to producers and consumers, and the project of keeping humanity distracted and divided.

This same impulse was behind my obsession with productivity, perfection, and performance. It was the framework I was living under. Though I had already spent much of my life and work breaking free from and combatting this approach, its residue was still there, still guiding how I moved through the world, what I valued, and my understanding of what it meant to be loved and accepted.

The truth was that my masks were inherited from a much more massive project, one that aggressively works to keep us dulled and distracted, stratified against each other, and estranged from the fullness and wonder of life. It is the nature of this *Possession-Control-Mastery* program to make everyone less human—not only those who are oppressed. Because oppression oppresses the oppressor too, diminishing our common humanity and separating us from our natural human dignity and vitality.

It was both daunting and relieving to learn about the scope and scale of what had been continually trying to pull me into a fictional story of efficiency and extraction. On one hand, it meant that there were much more powerful forces standing in opposition to me shedding my masks and getting my heart back than I had realized. On the other hand, I was now equipped with a powerful insight that could show me the way home.

Saying *Yes* and continuing down the mythical, mystical, ritual road is, in fact, by the very nature of the journey, an act of resistance against the warring way of *Possession-Control-Mastery* and its dehumanizing effects. Walking the way home is an embodiment of the vision of the biblical prophet Isaiah, echoed in the African American spiritual "Down by the Riverside," which declares, "I ain't gonna study war no more." It is, instead, to be a student of wholeness, belonging, and peace.

I was grateful for the opportunity to receive wisdom from these teachers through the vehicle of the podcast. But you don't have to start a podcast. That's not the point. What is important to remember is that in addition to soul friendship and spiritual direction or therapy, *Help* can also arrive in less personal forms like reading books, watching films, and listening to podcasts. All you need to do is pay attention to wisdom in any way it approaches you.

What a Guide Is Not (a List)

Now that we've explored possibilities about what the *anam cara* kind of *Help* looks like, let's take a moment to distinguish it from other forms of support that might be necessary in certain areas of your life, but which can also interfere with the journey.

A guide who helps you get your heart back:

- Does not tell you what to do or make decisions for you, e.g., *God has a plan for you and let me tell you exactly what it is!* Instead, they hold space for your soul to engage the swirling questions.
- Does not fixate on your problems and how to get rid of them, like certain pathology-centered approaches to therapy. Rather, the guide helps you move toward wholeness.
- Does not do the work for you. Put differently, you can't live vicariously through their life and practice. While you may glean generative insights from a pastor, podcast host, or mindfulness app guru who shares about what they have discovered on their journey, you need to move on from their mythology and make your own. True *Help* keeps you as the main character in your story.
- Does not focus on external success. This is not a business coach helping you to rebrand your life, sell yourself, or increase your influence. (Just buy their product or sign up

for their program!). This guide helps you wade into the depths of your soul in search of who you are and why you are here. Getting your heart back is the true treasure they want to help you find.

- Does not prioritize your stability and security, such as how you'll make a living or where you'll live or what you'll eat for dinner. This is not a protective parent, who naturally has these concerns for you. This person does not tell you to play it safe, but entices you to play with risk—and celebrates when you do!

- Does not allow you to avoid pain. This is not a cheerleader who just smiles and shouts, "Be positive!" This guide is a doula. It's gonna hurt like hell, they know, but they'll be there by your side the whole time as you push, reminding you to breathe and calling forth your courage and power.

This guiding work of *anam cara* is especially expressed by spiritual directors, but overlaps with a variety of modalities, such as therapy, mentoring, coaching, friendship—or at least the best expressions of these. But it cannot be reduced to any one of them. To be clear, it's also true that the best expressions of these roles incorporate aspects of *anam cara,* and often end up serving as catalysts for the soul journey.

Help Is the Path

In an ancient Buddhist story from the *Upaddha Sutta,* Ananda, the Buddha's devoted attendant and disciple, shares a reflection while sitting with his master.

"The way I see it, *half* of the spiritual life is nourishing friendship—accompanying and being accompanied by others," he says.

He's speaking about the power of the *sangha,* the community devoted to the path of the Buddha. Sangha is viewed as *one* of the *three* jewels of Buddhism, along with the Buddha himself and the dharma—the teaching and practice that make up the path, respectively.

So when Ananda says friendship is "half of the spiritual life," he is giving it a lot of credit. He thinks he's elevating its significance—it's not just a *third,* it's a *half!* Perhaps Ananda is confidently waiting for the Buddha to celebrate his brilliant insight.

But instead the Buddha corrects him:

"Not so, Ananda! This is the *entire* spiritual life."

Good friendship, the *kalyana mitra* kind of *Help,* the *anam cara* kind of companionship . . . This is not just an optional add-on to the way home.

It is much more than that.

It is *the way.*

"When I let go of what I am, I become what I might be. When I let go of what I have, I receive what I need."

—Lao Tzu

"We must be willing to get rid of the life we've planned, so as to have the life that is waiting for us. The old skin has to be shed before the new one can come."

—Joseph Campbell,
Reflections on the Art of Living

3

LET GO

As a Dog Returns to Its Vomit

As a dog returns to its vomit, so fools repeat their folly, an ancient proverb says. Humans don't always get things right the first time. Or the second or third time, for that matter. And, for many, this is often the case during the entire phase of Leaving the familiar. We are drawn back to what seems easier on the surface. We find our way to the path of least resistance. We hit the snooze button a few more times because we aren't quite ready to endure the challenges we must face.

Like Peter, who denied knowing his friend and teacher Jesus three times in an attempt to avoid similar suffering, I also refused three times to firmly embrace my call because I was afraid of what it might cost me. The first time I sold my soul for success in the eyes of others. Then *If you don't have your heart you have nothing* saved me. The second time, as I reverted to tying who I am to what I do, the *Help* of *anam caras* came and rescued me. And now, three years after this all began, I foolishly began to repeat the same folly.

My podcast project was steadily growing and gaining attention. As it neared one hundred episodes, I was thinking this was my next big thing. Maybe, I thought, I could turn this side project into something that could rescue me from my dreaded job. I decided to expand and rebrand it. I pushed past my tiredness and started plotting my next steps. It was time to get my hustle on.

But then one day all of my heartless scheming was interrupted. Again.

Get Quiet

Cherie and I were walking around the nearby university campus. As we exited the ornate, Hogwarts-style library and strolled past the gorgeous cherry blossoms we were there to witness, I was in my own world. I was thinking about the work I needed to do in order to make this a successful venture. Like a kid in a candy shop I was greedily pointing to the possibilities. *I'll do this. And then this. And then that.* But then I snapped out of my own world and slowed down for just a minute, looked at Cherie, and asked, "What do you think about all of this? What would you say to me as I move forward?"

She paused. She took a few breaths.

"Get quiet," she said.

"I think you need to get quiet."

Get quiet . . . They were Cherie's words, but it was the same voice that had been chasing me down across the years. The voice beckoning me back to come home. Telling me not to be afraid. Urging me to let go—and to *remain in the letting go.*

In each previous iteration of this moment, I did let go, at least, momentarily. But then I relapsed and returned to my masks soon after. Or I let go of one thing, but held on to multiple other things that I wasn't ready to surrender. Or I let go, but then reflexively latched on to something new. This time, however, I sensed a finality to the invitation to let go. At last, I understood: I had to really, truly leave home. And it was terrifying.

To conclude the process of Leaving, I needed to let go like a flying trapeze artist. With no wires above or nets below. And, actually, even less! I had to let go *without an approaching bar to grab*. And *without a high-flying partner to catch me*.

To *remain in the letting go*, that's what you need to do. You must release your grip, launch yourself into midair, and stay suspended there. Unable to go back to where you came from and with no guarantees of anything to come.

Crossing the Threshold

Letting go, the final step of Leaving the familiar, is the process of crossing the threshold between the supposed safety, security, and stability of the village and the uncertainty, shadows, and strangeness of the wild, uncharted lands beyond. It is a movement from the known to the unknown.

Just as Odysseus sets sail across the sea where Poseidon will violently throw his ship off course and just as Jesus resolutely sets out for Jerusalem where he will be arrested, tortured, and executed, once you cross the threshold there is no turning back. You pass the point of no return. You must burn the boats on the beach. You must blow up the bridges. The gate to your former life becomes locked shut behind you, but this is the only way to enter a new realm filled with power and possibility, a place that holds the keys to getting your heart back.

The threshold boundary is a powerful place, teeming with dangerous energy. It takes courage to cross. It also takes time. Sometimes passage through the threshold is brief. Bill Wilson, the founder of AA mentioned earlier, had a religious experience, and let go of alcohol forever. Paul's conversion from persecuting to preaching the way of Jesus was complete just a few days after a blinding vision on the road to Damascus. But often, passage is lengthy. Knowing this difference exists is critical. Because you don't want to fool yourself into thinking that you've done all the letting go you need to do.

For example, when things started to shift in my life after *If you don't have your heart, you have nothing,* it didn't take long for me to think that I was now, officially, wide awake—thank you very much! In reality, however, the threshold of my letting go spanned more than three years of my life. Old habits die hard. I just wouldn't stop holding on to the Impostor versions of myself.

Like most people, I expected something more instantaneous. I wanted the movie version of *Fellowship of the Ring* where Frodo sneaks out of the Shire shortly after his Call to Adventure arrives when he inherits the ring on Bilbo's eleventy-first birthday. But what I got was more like the original book version where he doesn't depart the safety of the Shire until a whole *seventeen years* later!

Regardless of whether you have a short or long runway for letting go, as you get closer to the crossing a new intensity and urgency enters your life. The volume in the conversation between your inside world and the outside world gets turned up. Let's look at two dynamics that signal that completing the threshold crossing is imminent.

Letting Go, with a Twist

First, you know you are close to crossing when you gain clarity about what precisely you need to let go of.

When Cherie told me to *get quiet* amid my frantic planning for my podcast and work, it wasn't just an invitation to thoughtful discernment about what I would do next, the message was a literal one. It meant that it was time to turn off the microphone. Not to build the project, but to end it. And this ending had a deeper meaning. It was about severing from my incessant need for projects and roles, achievements, and the approval of others to define who I am.

This is what the threshold requires. You are asked to let go of something specific that is an expression of the false identity that is hindering you. The particular thing is one symbolic iteration of the pattern that is limiting your life.

When you reach this point in your journey, you've grown in your awareness of the masks you've been wearing throughout your life. You've likely even shed some of them. But this doesn't mean it is easy to give up the charade. Your Impostor often resists in a last-gasp attempt to keep you stuck in the way things have always been.

That's why it is essential to watch out for misdirection. Your Impostor might try to insist that letting go must involve some grand gesture. Quitting your job, ending a struggling relationship, or moving across the country. Yes, that might be the thing that you finally need to have the courage to do, but it could equally be a form of avoidance. It might initially feel satisfying, but ultimately distract from the real issues at hand. You might need to do a bit more digging. Because this is less about letting go of a life situation, and more about letting go of the operating patterns that you bring to those situations. This is why letting go usually involves a twist—it's not the obvious thing that needs to go; it's the more subtle thing.

For example, letting go might actually require that you stop doing something you enjoy. Maybe, in order to confront your need to be needed, it's finally time to stop playing counselor with your friends or to take a break from all of the volunteering and serving you do in the community.

Or maybe your letting go means staying with something that is hard. It's time to let go of your pattern of avoidance—how you always move on to the next person or place when things get difficult. Perhaps it's time to stick around and work through the conflict for a change.

Letting go can also relate to moving on from something that has been challenging and necessary but has run its course. Like grief or celebration that has trapped you in your own repetitive Groundhog Day, a creative project that is dragging on, or a particular health routine that has become obsessive.

Maybe you need to remove the mask of passivity that you use to justify your victim status or, conversely, depart from the domineering ways you show up in relationships. Whatever it is, letting go often requires you to be more creative than you think.

You usually know you are letting go of the thing you need to when you are not just *turning away* from something, but *turning toward* something. When you are not just *escaping* a perpetual issue in your life, but *engaging* it.

As for my letting go, I wanted to quit my job. While it allowed me to help some organizations and leaders that were making generative, compassionate contributions to their communities, I also had to deal with the kind of bullshit that was the antithesis of everything I understood the way of Jesus to be about: arrogant religiosity, false piety, obsession with certainty, hateful exclusion, and much more. I wasn't naive about these streaks in my religious tradition—or any religious tradition for that matter—but in my work as a pastor I had intentionally steered clear from this toxicity and instead leaned into other foundational, yet too often forgotten, elements of the Christ story. The reason I was a part of it all was to lean into the mystery of being human, build belonging, and work for justice. But this job forced me into contexts where I was around people who weren't there for the same reasons, people who were perpetuating the harmful, ugly aspects of religion. Being up close to this stuff after years of orbiting far, far away from institutional religion was suffocating. But it also clarified my sense that I didn't want to be a part of the whole enterprise anymore, that I was no longer interested in fighting for change from the inside, and that it actually had been many years earlier that my spirituality had outgrown the container that once upon a time had nurtured my growth.

Clearly, there was a lot going on for me with the job. It stirred up strong feelings, which I would have to face eventually. But it wasn't to blame for all my problems. It wasn't ground zero for my issues. Leaving it would have been an empty gesture. Because the real issue I needed to let go of was my pattern of forming unhealthy attachments to the work I do and trying to gain love and acceptance for the roles I play and the things I accomplish.

And that's how I found myself in the kind of plot twist that letting go often presents: it wasn't the job I *didn't like* that I needed to leave, but the podcast project I *did like* that needed to go. In fact, ending the project *and* staying in the job were *both* expressions of the letting go that I needed to do. Both acts confronted my Impostor's obsession with roles, affiliations, and achievements. Both exposed me to the discomfort and vulnerability of not having a mask to hide behind. And both gave me the opportunity to see more of my true face.

Entering Dreamtime

The second indication that you are crossing the threshold is that you feel like you are entering a new realm. An area charged with mystery, imagination, possibility, and connection. You begin to experience the magical energy of the zone of the unknown. While you're not solidly in this realm until you let go, you can feel its magnetic pull.

It's difficult to describe . . . But there is an electricity in the air. You start to sense the soul of the world. You flow through time in a different way.

The Aboriginal Australian people have a beautiful term they use to describe when the world was created by the Ancestral Spirits: *Dreamtime*. It refers to the time when the Ancestral Spirits created life, how things moved from a subjective, spiritual state to an objective, material expression. It's not just in the past; it's also here and now. Dreamtime is when all new and creative possibilities emerge. Dreamtime is where everything is interconnected.

What you experience as you approach the threshold is a sort of dreamtime. Something is being created. Everything seems to flow together. Your dreams feel awake. Your waking state feels like dreaming. It is a sign that the Impostor is about to lose its grip. Its resistance is diminishing. Your imagination is no longer drawn to distracting desires or illusions about what matters, but to *the real*.

After Cherie told me to get quiet, I did. I pulled the plug on my project. And for the first time I didn't have anything to pour myself into. I discovered that things get *really* quiet when you let go. According to Lisa Miller's research into spirituality and the brain, part of what was happening, neurologically speaking, is that I was quieting my "achievement awareness," my top-down, detail-focused perception. As a result, my "awakened awareness," or bottom-up perception, had space to expand. When I let go of my achievement obsession, symbolized by the podcast, I became more open. I was curious. I was constantly listening.

And almost immediately I began to experience the connection and flow and intensity that were spilling over from the zone of the unknown I was transitioning into.

I'm on a work trip in New Mexico, sitting in prayerful silence with Franciscan priest Father Richard Rohr and his community. A woman there tells me about an intriguing podcast and next I'm listening to it as I drive across Route 66. It's a discussion about evolving spiritually, and it mentions the Indigenous practice of the vision quest and the same book that a friend recommended to me months earlier. It's exactly what I need to hear.

Then I am in a remote Native American pueblo for a work consultation. A man approaches me and points to the other side of the bridge that crosses a dried-up creek bed. Out of a small doorway, one by one, fifty men, masked and in full ceremonial costume, emerge singing and dancing. They are kachina dancers and these are the harvest dances, the man explains. He leads me up to a rooftop over a hidden village square. A warm desert wind swirls around me. In the distance I see a dilapidated three-hundred-year-old Spanish Catholic chapel. And, in front of me, as the dancers enter the square in their vibrant colors, I witness a sacred ritual that calls forth within me aliveness and resilience, gratitude and growth.

Next I am driving on a winding road between the canyon walls, spontaneously singing songs of hope. Longing, like the kachina dancers, for the harvest—the harvest in my own life.

Suddenly I'm back home, sipping a beer and reading the book recommended by my friend and the Route 66 podcast. It's called Soulcraft, and I'm enthralled by every word about soul and nature, about descending to the underworld and encountering the animal world.

Then, as I hike alone in the Cascade Mountains, I'm wondering what animal I might encounter in the forest. Ascending the steep trail and descending back to my car in the parking lot, I have this strange sense that a cougar is watching me. The following day I read the tragic news of a rare cougar attack of two mountain bikers a few miles away.

Now I'm asleep in my parents' basement. I fall into a deep dream, and I'm terrified as I stand face-to-face with a ferocious, large cat—my threshold guardian.

Guardian at the Gate

We will get back to the dream, but first: *What in the world is a threshold guardian?*

To cross the threshold into a new realm of life, the mythical hero must face the threshold guardian. It is an intimidating force that stands at the boundary between the ordinary world and the sacred realm of soul. Between the status quo and the dynamic unknown.

In many traditions, the guardian stands at the entrance to the temple to scare off any traveler who is not capable of encountering the power and wisdom within, like the cherubim guarding the tabernacle's Holy of Holies. The imposing presence of the threshold guardian wards off those who aren't yet ready to leave behind their dependency on the noise and activity of life as they've known it.

But just because many choose to go no farther when confronted with the fierce and intimidating presence doesn't mean the guardian is dangerous. In fact, to anyone who has the courage to choose above all else to reclaim their heart, the guardian is a source of support. It's just as the King of Salem tells Santiago the shepherd boy in *The Alchemist*. A magical force arrives as you continue your journey. It may appear to be negative, but it actually shows you what to do to get your heart back. What seems to be a menace is ultimately an ally.

The Greek god Pan is the typical example of the threshold guardian. Pan lived in the woodlands beyond the village. Many who stumbled beyond the safe boundary of the village into Pan's domain would be overwhelmed with fear at the slightest sound of rustling leaves or creaking branches—this is where the term *panic* comes from—and flee from the scene in terror. But Pan was harmless, and even generous, to those who approached with reverence, providing abundant food, health, and wisdom.

Your threshold guardian, however, isn't likely a half-human, half-goat running around the woods. But who can say?

It may be one final expression of what you need to let go of. Or it might be a symbol of that letting go—in a dream, with an animal, or in a run-in with another person. Fundamentally, your threshold guardian is *misattributed power*. It is a person or situation or story or system to which you've relinquished power when in fact you hold the power. You've been ignoring your power, but you've had it all along.

It is the failure that terrifies you, but which actually leads to self-discovery and new creative possibilities. The appointment for the nagging physical issue you've been putting off that ends up pointing you in the direction of your future health and strength. The colleague you've been avoiding who turns out to be a powerful source of wisdom and encouragement.

The threshold guardian takes many forms.

Mine came to me in a dream in my parents' basement.

Return of the Jaguar

A couple weeks after New Mexico I was in Chicago for meetings. Before flying home, I had a one-night window so I decided to drive up to my parents' cottage to see them.

That night I slept on a pullout couch in the basement.

Despite the dreamlike nature of my waking life during that time, I had not remembered a dream in the longest time. Until that night.

I'm walking around a dusty, abandoned old house.

I notice a glass panel, floor to ceiling, in the corner of the living room.

I can see a lush, green forest on the other side, but as I approach the window, I stop in fear . . .

There's something out there.

Suddenly, a massive jaguar is thrashing up against the glass, baring its huge teeth and swinging its sharp claws.

I'm frozen.

Even though I'm protected by the glass and the walls of the house, I can't move. I'm convinced that if I don't keep my eyes on this huge cat, it will crush my skull with its canines or kill me with a single swipe.

Hours pass, maybe days. Eventually, I muster the courage to take my eyes off the jaguar. I allow myself to move. And I explore the house. I go upstairs. The rooms have abandoned desks and dressers, but nothing else. I go into the garage. Just some empty shelves. I look around the rest of the house, and it's nothing but cobwebs and a few rotting cardboard boxes.

Then I return to the living room window—and the jaguar is gone!

Strangely, I'm not afraid. I'm calm.

I'm no longer worried that the jaguar is in the house.

Instead, I'm inspired by the jaguar's leaving.

There's no reason for me to stay in this dead, dilapidated house.

There's nothing here for me.

Even though it means walking out into the wild where this ferocious beast could in fact stalk and kill me, I fear nothing.

It's time for me to leave too.

I go to the garage. I press the button and the garage door slowly opens. Sunlight and the sounds of a thousand living things come pouring in.

Pure joy fills my heart as I walk out of the house and into the dense jungle, teeming with life.

Into the wild.

And then I woke up.

Dreamwork

The prominence of dreams in ancient literature suggests that for as long as human beings have been dreaming we have probably also been trying to make meaning of our dreams.

In one of the earliest surviving texts, Gilgamesh sees an ax fall from the sky, symbolizing the arrival of a powerful person. Pharaoh dreams of seven skinny cows devouring seven fat cows, which Joseph interprets as a seven-year famine following seven years of abundance. Zeus sends a dream to the Greek commander Agamemnon during the Trojan War to go to battle.

For generations, Native American tribes have created dream catchers to retain and repel good and bad dreams, respectively. Meanwhile, Muslim scholars produced extensive writings on dream interpretation during the Middle Ages. And, much later, a young Swiss boy named Carl Jung dreamed of a turd descending from the throne of God and shattering the roof of a cathedral.

Jung's work on dreams would later eclipse the pioneering dream analysis approach of Sigmund Freud, whose work, famously, was more sexually preoccupied. Jung saw dreams as an expression of the unconscious mind. As such, they are a tool to solve problems in one's waking life. While dreams are a source of creativity and may delve into the past or anticipate the future, the main task of making meaning of dreams lies in interpreting the symbols that a dream carries.

Whether our dreams include more common elements like teeth falling out or standing naked in front of a crowd, or more obscure scenarios, dreamwork is a powerful tool that assists in keeping the dream alive, so that its meanings—which seek to deliver wellbeing and wholeness—can continue to unfold in your life. Black Elk, a Lakota holy man, said that dreams are the way that the Great Spirit, Wakan Tanka, often delivers the most powerful visions for our lives. As such, dreams provide a steady flow of invaluable information when it comes to finding your way home.

I had the dream.

Now I needed to do some dreamwork.

Revisiting the Dream

A few weeks before the jaguar dream, I had made the decision that after a year of meeting with Tall Tim, I would be concluding my spiritual direction sessions with him. I was getting quiet, as per Cherie's instructions, and felt like I was in a decent place. I planned to tell him at our next session. But when I had the dream, I wanted to see Tall Tim as soon as possible. I needed to process my experience and figure out what it meant.

When we met up for a session in a small chapel on a local Jesuit university campus, I told him about the dream right away.

"Would you like to explore the dream a bit more?" he asked.

I nodded, and he asked me to close my eyes.

He invited me to go back into the house in my imagination and, if I was comfortable, to share what I was experiencing.

I enter the house. It's really quiet.

I slowly walk toward the glass panel.

I can see the jaguar. It is lying calmly on the ground.

I sit down quietly. The jaguar is watching me. We stare into each other's eyes.

In an instant, the glass panel—between the jaguar and me, between the safety of the house and the danger of the wild—dissolves. And now, all the sudden, I'm holding the jaguar gently in my arms.

That's where my revisitation of the dream ended.

I opened my eyes and started laughing because the whole spooning-with-a-jaguar thing reminded me of an old Siegfried & Roy magic act or something. Tall Tim chuckled with me.

"Is there anything you think this dream is saying to you?" he asked.

I began to speak and it all just came flowing out of me . . .

That the jaguar and I are connected. That we are one. That it was never trying to threaten me, but it was always trying to get my attention because it had an urgent message to deliver: that I have to leave behind the identity that I built, that I have to let go of the belief that I'm only loveable if I act a certain way or achieve certain things. The jaguar was thrashing around because it was trying to tell me that I have to get the fuck out of that deteriorating old house!

As I worked through the dream with Tall Tim, my initial impression from the dream was confirmed and strengthened. After all the ways I had been answering the call and getting help and, most recently, refusing to once again confuse my identity with my work, the dream symbolized that a deep psychological shift had indeed taken place:

I let go.

I crossed the threshold from the known into the unknown.

I entered the next phase of the grand quest to get my heart back.

Just as Jaguar in its car motto form in my *Grace, Space, Pace* encounter was an ally to trust, so too was the intimidating jaguar in my dream. A force that was for me, not against me. Emboldening me to do something that is at the core of all mystical experience—to leave the old ways behind, to set out from the familiar so I could discover who I am and why I'm here.

Not only that, but the jaguar was a reflection of myself. The glass panel was a mirror. And the image of my arms wrapped around the jaguar was a symbol of oneness. The dream was showing me that I would need to awaken to my own "jaguar-ness" to navigate the wild terrain in front of me.

Tall Tim celebrated my discoveries and encouraged me to keep paying attention to my dreams. I would continue to have his support as I worked with my dreams, but he offered me three simple tips that support one's own personal dreamwork:

1. Before you go to bed, ask the "dreammaker" (or whatever you want to call it) to visit you in your sleep.

2. Keep a dream journal next to your bed and write down what you remember as soon as you wake up (and wake up slowly, by the way).

3. Reflect on any associations you may have with the dream images—the people, places, scenarios, etc. *What message or messages is this dream communicating to you?* Or as a guide

on a wilderness quest later articulated, *What shimmers? Where is it alive? Let it live!*

Vision Quest

After we finished exploring the dream, I told Tall Tim about some of the other things that had recently happened. How I felt pulled to wild places. About the cougar attack close to where I had just been hiking. And about my enchanted New Mexico trip, and how both the podcast I listened to on Route 66 and the book it mentioned, *Soulcraft,* had brought up the practice of the *vision quest.* I had heard of it before, but now I was especially intrigued.

Vision quest is a term that refers to rite of passage ceremonies from Indigenous cultures around the world that mark the transition from childhood into adulthood and full participation in the community. The Lakota word *hanbleceya,* from which *vision quest* is derived, literally means "crying for a dream" or "lamenting for a dream." In these ceremonies, young people are sent away from the community for a period of time in which they suffer, undergo a spiritual death, and cry out for a vision for their lives and their people. Afterward, they return to their communities with clarity about their contribution, ready to serve their people and offer their gift. A *vision quest,* at its core, is a ritual that enacts the pattern of *Leaving, Falling, Rising.*

Every time I came across the concept, I felt a deep longing stirring within me. I was so inspired by the wisdom and power in this Indigenous practice. I lamented having no context for this in my culture. But it was something I wanted to do. I wanted to be cut off from my community, to be alone in the wild, to cry out for a dream. I wanted to go on a vision quest.

So that's what I told Tall Tim near the end of that spiritual direction session:

"I need to go on a vision quest."

He nodded. He could sense my yearning. He knew I wanted to be alone, in the wild, pushing my edges. He knew that I wanted to keep growing. But what this *anam cara* said was the most important thing—a reminder I will always have with me about not relying on or waiting for some external element or process to facilitate transformation in my life. What he said kept me in the present moment, and it kept me in my own power.

It may or may not have happened like this, but as I remember it now, Tall Tim gently waved his hand in the air and responded to me in Yoda-like fashion:

"On a vision quest, you already are."

The words reverberated within me and I felt chills all over my body.

He was right. The jaguar dream. *Get quiet.* Before that, having the courage to leave my job, which resulted from the practices of *Grace, Space, Pace.* And stretching all the way back to the *If you don't have your heart, you have nothing* invitation on that rainy morning run. It was all connected, with each new encounter spurring me onward, downward toward soul, toward getting my heart back. It was all part of the same journey. I didn't need to wait to get out into the wild, or for solitude and fasting. Because I was already on a vision quest. I had been for years.

Tall Tim could tell that I was resonating with what he said. He then gently clarified that it's best to reserve the term *vision quest* for the particular practice of Indigenous communities out of respect. But he affirmed that the *quest* or *soul quest* or *wilderness quest* template was for me too. That it is for everyone. According to Richard Erdoes' account in *Crying for a Dream,* Sioux holy man John Lame Deer saw the *hanbleceya* as the beginning of all religion. It's visible in the desert activities of the Hebrew prophets and later John the Baptist and Jesus. A version shows up in ancient Greece at Eleusis during the annual rites of the cult of Demeter and Persephone too. A form of this practice exists in countless cultural and religious traditions because just as people get guidance from dreams, people receive direction and gain clarity when they are sequestered from society for a season.

The quest is a template for all of humanity, but sadly, it's also a lost art for so many. Instead of going into the desert to surrender to divine love and discern how to care for our communities, we so often have chosen to pursue the *Possession-Control-Mastery* "virtues." As a result, our inner worlds become barren deserts where nothing grows. "A place without dreams or life," observed Lame Deer. That's why my heart was all dried out. I had allowed my allegiance to the selfish priorities of my Impostor to shut out the voice of the divine.

But not anymore. Tall Tim knew that I had been doing the hard work, digging deep to find the soul water of the desert spring. He saw that my inner desert was becoming green again. I knew it too. Sometimes, as in this particular spiritual direction session, I could even feel the early sprouting of the dense jungle—like the one the jaguar disappeared into in my dream—that would one day be within me.

He encouraged my desire to someday go on a literal wilderness quest where I would experience isolation and fasting—and one year later, drenched in rain and walking alone in a dark canyon, I would be doing exactly that. But in the meantime, the invitation Tall Tim gave me to see my present-day journey through the lens of the ancient *vision quest* gave me courage to continue onward, which I clung to whenever critical voices would rise up within me: *Isn't all of this inner work a bit self-absorbed? Isn't this focus on yourself privileged? Aren't there more pressing issues than getting your heart back? Racism and inequity? Poverty and hunger? Climate catastrophe? Shouldn't you be doing something more worthwhile?*

In these moments, I rested in the wisdom of those who had gone before me. This quest wasn't a distraction. It wasn't an escape. I was, in fact, making my greatest contribution to humanity—to know my true self. I was not stepping away from the world's pressing problems. I was engaging them by becoming more whole, and preparing to be an even more generative and sustainable healing presence in the world. However others have come to misappropriate the term *vision quest*, this is what has always been at its heart: it's not about yourself; it's about giving your life as a gift of love and service to your people and the planet.

I left the spiritual direction session and my spirit was soaring. I was so energized by exploring the jaguar dream and talking about the quest I was on, and then a couple of "coincidences" immediately confirmed what Tall Tim had said.

As soon as I exited the chapel, I overheard a random snippet from the conversation the people in front of me were having: "My sister keeps big cats in her garage."

Seriously? My dream was about a big, domesticated cat finally leaving a home, and me—mysteriously one with that jaguar—departing through the garage.

A few blocks later I turned my head and saw a jaguar statue

covered in jewels staring back at me from the other side of a tall storefront window.

A jaguar behind a panel of glass. Just like my dream.

Later that night, I picked up Bill Plotkin's *Soulcraft* and read:

"Crossing that threshold into your uncharted future is an act of great courage and self-compassion, and it changes your relationship to life in a fundamental way. It embodies your willingness to employ a new form of risk-taking, to consciously choose growth-stimulating, soul-nourishing conflicts, to live through the accompanying anxiety, and to accept your life as open-ended and unpredictable. Passing through that door commits you to living in the present in a way you never have before. Your personal, cultural, or religious past no longer provides you with a map to your future."

The words resonated deeply.

They reminded me of the words of Gandalf. When you let go, "Things are now in motion that cannot be undone."

I felt relief and gratitude for letting go. The Leaving years were long years. But essential. Because I needed all that time to shake off my stubborn Impostor. Later I would realize that this long season was also critical preparation for navigating the next phase of the journey.

But that afternoon, I was simply thrilled about the new world opening in front of me.

That whole day I felt like I was flying.

What I didn't realize yet is that I was actually falling.

Into the unknown.

PHASE TWO
Falling into the Unknown

A few days after revisiting my jaguar dream with Tall Tim, I was still soaring. A heavy burden had been lifted. I felt free. Leaving the familiar was exhilarating and filled me with the possibility of newness. But it didn't take long for the reality of Falling into the unknown to set in, with its abundance of challenges, trials, and obstacles. In fact, almost immediately I had an experience that foreshadowed what the next season of my life would entail.

One morning I missed the bus for a downtown meeting. I scrambled to borrow my friend's car, but I was convinced I would still be late. Somehow I cruised downtown through Seattle morning traffic in record time and landed a parking spot right outside the cafe. It was a miracle! As I pulled my parking slip from the machine, I was thrilled with my good fortune, as if it resembled the successful escape I had just made from the previous version of my life.

But in an instant, it all changed.

A heavy splatter from the sky blasted my hand, my head, my chest, my shoes. I was thoroughly covered in pigeon shit. I froze, and just then a man who lived on the streets walked by me and smiled. Without missing a beat, he said, "That means you have good luck today. That's what they say. You should go to a casino or something." Then he noticed my hair, "Oh, it's even on your head. That means you are really, really lucky!"

Ultimately, the man was correct. To leave the deteriorating home of the first half of life is to hit the jackpot. But the prize of rebirth is never quickly realized. It is a long, winding road filled with initiatory challenges and emboldening revelations. At each turn there is another castle wall to scale or dragon to defeat, over and over again.

You must now travel on *the road of trials.*

You must walk through *the valley of the shadow of death.*

You must pass through *the underworld.*

This is the nature of the Falling into the unknown phase: it is where you become engulfed in darkness, get lost in the wild, and meet your mortality.

In other words, it's a bit of a shit show.

Which is why the pigeon's airstrike was so prophetic.

It was a warning sign for all that happened next.

And perhaps, in the same way that it rattled my composed appearance as I stepped into my morning meeting, the bird shit was also cheekily posing the critical question that Campbell says is still hanging in the balance at this point: *Can the ego put itself to death?*

"Leave the door open for the unknown, the door into the dark. That's where the most important things come from, where you yourself came from, and where you will go."

—Rebecca Solnit,
A Field Guide to Getting Lost

"The dark night of the soul comes just before revelation. When everything is lost, and all seems darkness, then comes the new life and all that is needed."

—Joseph Campbell,
Reflections on the Art of Living

4

BEFRIEND THE DARKNESS

Tombs and Wombs

A descent into darkness.

This is the common experience that characters endure throughout the old stories.

And it is an unavoidable part of the quest for anyone who wishes to get their heart back.

Myths often convey the reality of descending into darkness through the image of the belly of the beast. In one of the most well-known versions of the pattern, the prophet Jonah gets tossed overboard and swallowed by a whale. In another, Maui dies when trying to enter the body of the massive goddess of the underworld through her vagina and exit through her mouth. Little Red Riding Hood, meanwhile, ends up in the wolf's stomach before cutting herself out with a pair of scissors. (I feel like the gory scissors part of the story was clipped out of the version I heard as a kid).

Regardless of where the hero precisely is anatomically, this belly image represents the darkness, a place of uncertainty, disorientation, and restlessness. A place where, by all accounts, you cease to exist—at least the person you and everyone else once knew you to be.

Of course, darkness isn't just about the *end* of something, as the belly image suggests. Across time and place, darkness is about *beginnings* too. So, yes, the darkness that you find yourself in after Leaving the familiar is a *tomb*. But it's also a *womb*.

That's why many spiritual traditions include stories of people entering the womb-like darkness of caves in their quest to become more human, more alive. The Buddha meditated in caves, and today meditation caves can be found across India, China, and Tibet. Hindu gurus spent a lot of time meditating in caves too, including a legendary king who slept in a cave for four million years. Muhammad's destination for solitude was a cave. From the darkness of that womb, the first verses of the Qur'an were born. Jesus emerged from the darkness of a cave three days after his crucifixion.

It's true for Tony Stark of the Marvel Cinematic Universe too. After being abducted, it is a dark cave that serves as the location of his transformation from egotistical arms dealer to slightly less egotistical, sort-of-humanitarian, Iron Man.

Across these stories, caves are wombs. They are places where people are reborn. Understanding this connection, early Mexican civilizations built caves resembling wombs beneath pyramids. Chinese tradition also seemed to understand the mysterious, transformative power of caves. According to religious historian Mircea Eliade in *Rites and Symbols of Initiation*, "The Chinese term *dong*, 'cave,' finally came to have the meaning 'mysterious, profound, transcendent.'" And Spanish cave paintings that were created sixty-five thousand years ago suggest that even before *Homo sapiens* got the idea, Neanderthals were going into the darkness to seek and create meaning.

This meaning-making activity has been true in the darkness outside of caves too—from the honoring of the dark across cultures at the winter solstice to the now-discouraged Dutch "dropping" tradition, a rite of passage in which groups of preteens are left in the woods in the middle of the night and have to find their way home.

Priest and author Barbara Brown Taylor, who says darkness gets a bad rap in *Learning to Walk in the Dark*, sums up the role darkness plays across all of these stories: "New life starts in the dark. Whether it is a seed in the ground, a baby in the womb, or Jesus in the tomb, it starts in the dark."

Remember this when you are plunged into the darkness: *New life starts in the dark.* Because as all these stories indicate, the darkness will come for you. You don't have to swim out to sea in search of Shamu. You don't have to crawl into an underground cave to find it. The darkness will find you. On your Monday morning commute. In the bleachers at your kid's Little League baseball game. In the comfort of your own living room. It will find you and it will consume you. Externally, you might look completely normal to the outside world. But internally, you will be traversing through a dark, seemingly endless passage.

You will be tempted to ignore the darkness or flee from it in fear. But you need to remain in the darkness. To stay present to it. Because as you fall into the unknown—your soul initiation— your unavoidable task is to befriend the darkness. When you befriend the darkness, which lies in the depths of who you are, you will discover that it is a nourishing dark, essential to your rebirth.

I wish I would have known this when I descended into the darkness.

Thor Thoughts

That spring, just after the jaguar began to stalk me in my dreams and beyond, I felt the creeping darkness for the first time. My son and I were making our way through the Marvel movies in chronological order and it was time to watch *Thor*, the cinematic story of the comic book character inspired by the figure from Norse mythology.

Thor is a powerful god, known for his mighty feats in battle, empowered by his thunderously powerful hammer, Mjolnir. But then he has a falling out with his father. Thor is stripped of his power and his hammer, and he is banished to earth.

Soon after landing on the planet, Thor ends up, as all bummed-out movie characters do, at a dive bar. Reflecting on his new situation over a couple cold ones, he says: "I had it all backwards. I had it all wrong. For the first time in my life, I have no idea what I'm supposed to do."

Snuggled up on the couch next to my son, I gasped. It struck a deep chord in me. It was exactly how I felt.

I had shed so many layers that, like Thor, I felt like I had lost my core powers. I no longer had the hammer that I depended on for my strength. My roles, my identities, my "secure" sense of self were all gone. I was stripped of everything that I identified as so central to me being "me." *I start things. I help people. I achieve. I organize. I get shit done. I impress.* But now that I was no longer defined by those things, where did I even fit in my community and in the world? I felt dissociated from my previous life.

The initial thrill of leaving the village and venturing out into the unknown had vanished. A new reality began to set in: complete disorientation. *What do I do? Where do I go?* I craved direction and clarity. I wanted a glimpse of what might be ahead. But there was no light at the end of the tunnel. There was no light at all. It was just a tunnel all the way down.

Dark Night of the Soul

John of the Cross, the sixteenth-century Spanish Catholic mystic and priest mentioned earlier, calls this experience the "dark night of the soul." The dark night of the soul comes when everything that used to work for you doesn't work anymore. It comes when you relinquish, eagerly or stubbornly, the patterns that you were attached to. Without the ways of showing up in the world that you once depended on, you experience a kind of *Impostor withdrawal*—empty, lost, confused, exhausted, and alone.

But, to be clear, this dark night of the soul doesn't arrive because you let go of the *negative* Impostor patterns that hindered or harmed you. The reason this dark night arrives is because even the *positive* things—the ways that used to work for you, even the things that brought you joy or connection to God and others—just don't work anymore. It's all expired. Meaningless. Rubbish. Because the monster that is your Impostor has had its tentacles wrapped around every area of your life this whole time. It isn't going to be thrown down into the abyss without pulling what remains of you down with it.

In my case, I knew I was casting off my former obsessions with achievement, perfection, and performing for the approval of others when I got quiet and shut down my podcast project. But I didn't realize what a firm grip they had on areas of my life that were generally healthy and strong: my relationships, vocation, and spirituality. As a result of Leaving the familiar, my sense of place in community and relationships was shattered. I retreated from my former extroverted ways into introversion. The rudder of my vocational life was torn off. My passion and courage vanished. In terms of my career, I felt like I had reached a dead end. And, most disorienting of all, my spirituality withered up. It had always been an intimate source of inspiration and imagination, but now it seemed as if my internal spiritual experience had been invaded and destroyed by the external religious system I had always protected myself against.

I felt like I had nothing to turn to. It was uncomfortable. It was lonely.

But this was exactly where I needed to be.

In her preface to John of the Cross' book *The Dark Night of the Soul,* wisdom teacher Mirabai Starr speaks to the opportunity the darkness gives us:

> "The dark night is about being fully present in the tender, wounded emptiness of our own souls. It's about not turning from the pain but learning to rest in it. Rather than distracting ourselves from the simple darkness at our core, we sit with it, paying close attention, and opening our hearts to all that is left, which is love."

In other words, we need to *befriend the darkness.* That's how we discover that the darkness is a teacher and healer. Darkness frees us from the prison of the false worlds we've constructed—the confining walls, floor, and ceiling of our Impostor disappear. Darkness helps us see our shadow, the parts of ourselves we judge as unacceptable—insecurities and fears, doubts and desires. Darkness enables us to escape from being externally referenced, from being reliant on the thoughts and judgments of others to define who we are. Darkness distills us into our essential identity.

Disoriented in the darkness, with nothing outside of yourself to grab onto and no future plans to escape to, you begin to become acquainted with the deep stillness that is at the core of your being: an abundant, loving, powerful presence, here and now.

That is your heart.

That is your home.

The dark night of the soul may manifest itself externally with any number of symptoms. Agitation or apathy. Sorrow or sluggishness. Pessimism or purposelessness. Ultimately, however, it is a solitary inner experience. And just as in any part of this entire journey, it is critical to turn to grounding and generative Ritual Practices—this is *how* we befriend the darkness. During my dark night of the soul, three practices assisted me: animal apprenticeship, creative expression through poetry, and a ritual called the death lodge.

Animal Apprenticeship

From the moment I left the spiritual direction session where I shared the jaguar dream with Tall Tim, jaguar connections—and cat connections in general—seemed to find me everywhere I went. Immediately, there was the big-cat-in-the-garage comment followed by the jaguar statue in the store window. But then I kept running into jaguar murals at restaurants and cat paintings in coffee shops. And I thought about how people always mispronounced my name as "cat," and laughed at how an old high school girlfriend had shouted, "Bob! Cat!" a few years earlier when we ran into each other after not seeing each other for fifteen years (I guess our love wasn't as true and strong as I thought . . . sigh!). I also thought about my daughter's jaguar tattoo suggestion that led to Grace, Space, Pace, about how friends' cats have always climbed up onto my lap, even though I am by no means a cat lover, and about how I woke up the morning after the initial jaguar dream with itchy eyes—the typical allergic reaction I have to cats—almost as if I had actually interacted with one during my sleep.

It might all have been a coincidence. Besides, aren't cats just everywhere? But it was intriguing to me. I couldn't help but sense that I was being stalked by the jaguar. So at my next session, I brought it up with Tall Tim.

"Is the jaguar my spirit animal?" I asked.

Just as he had done with the phrase vision quest, Tall Tim kindly offered a correction that the term spirit animal was getting thrown around recklessly in popular culture. The term, he suggested, should be reserved for Indigenous communities out of reverence for what this sacred idea means to them.

I understood what he meant. I had noticed that it had become trendy for people to use the term to describe something they really like. I told him I had recently seen a coffee mug that said, Coffee is my spirit animal. This was exactly the kind of flippant use to avoid, Tall Tim explained, but he affirmed my sense of a mystical connection with jaguars and cats.

"Animals are always showing up to help us," Tall Tim said, "especially when we open ourselves up to their guidance. Some people call it a *power animal* or *animal guide*. Sometimes it's a group, a *council of power animals*."

I listened attentively.

He added, "And you don't pick the animal, it picks you."

I was elated. "It could have been anything, like a hamster or possum," I joked, "but I lucked out and got a stealthy, ferocious, and mysterious jaguar as my guide!"

Tim was unfazed.

"So what should I do if I think the jaguar is my power animal?" I asked.

"You become an apprentice to the animal," Tall Tim answered. "An animal guide often serves as a mirror. The animal teaches you things about yourself that you can't see."

My Jaguar Journey

A few years after this conversation, I watched the documentary *My Octopus Teacher*. During a difficult time in his life, filmmaker Craig Foster begins to swim in the frigid waters of the South African shore he grew up on. One day, while snorkeling through the underwater kelp forest, he meets an octopus. Slowly, he builds a relationship with this octopus. With each encounter, not only does he learn something about the octopus, but he discovers more about himself. He becomes a student of the octopus, and it heals him.

Now I wasn't in a position to get this up close and personal with a jaguar. I wasn't going to move to the rainforests of Belize or Brazil to make myself available for a relationship with a jaguar. Nor did that sound like a very wise idea! But I did need to figure out how I could become a student of the jaguar even if the closest wild teacher was thousands of miles away. Tall Tim helped me identify dreams, books, and the zoo as the domain of my jaguar apprenticeship.

I was more than ready for some jaguar wisdom. I was growing increasingly restless each day. It was a new season of darkness, but in many ways the experience of disorientation stretched back years. I had slowly been descending into the darkness since my wake-up call.

On the work front, I still wanted out of the job I had been in for two years. The problem was, when I relinquished my achievement orientation, I lost all confidence in my skills. I felt like my best days were behind me. I was washed up. I had no sense of purpose. Financial stress magnified all these sentiments. I couldn't stay at my job and I couldn't leave either. I felt cornered.

The jaguar didn't have an answer for my exact situation, but it did offer reassurance.

In a fresh dream . . . *A jaguar is on the prowl. I am watching her from a distance, high above the valley where she walks. But then she finds me. Approaching me with strong and soft eyes, she silently says, "You've got this."*

It was a message that I was okay in my lostness, confusion, and emptiness. I didn't need to look to anything outside of myself to become more whole or to make things better. I was fine right where I was, and I had the inner fortitude to persevere in the not-knowing of how things would turn out for me.

The articles and books I read validated the jaguar's capacity to offer wisdom in the unknown that I had experienced in the dream. Some of them spoke of jaguar's role as an underworld guide—one who is at home in the mystery and unknown the darkness represents. In his book *An Indomitable Beast: The Remarkable Journey of the Jaguar*, Alan Rabinowitz, who established the world's first jaguar conservation area, highlighted the jaguar's audacious ability to survive. This apex predator's cleverness and resilience enabled it to endure the dramas of the Ice Age and everything that followed—pesky parasites, hunting humans, habitat loss, range contraction, and the depletion of prey. *Cats have nine lives,* they say.

Once Rabinowitz asked an experienced zookeeper to describe jaguars, specifically as they compare to other big cats.

"Alert, confident, persistent, efficient," the zookeeper answered without hesitation.

"What do you mean by efficient?" Rabinowitz asked.

"Like a long-distance athlete," the zookeeper replied. "If a jaguar moves, something is going on and he is going to get what he wants."

These literary jaguar encounters energized me. Jaguar was teaching me of my own innate capacity for patience and perseverance in the face of challenges. I was made for this long, dark night.

Beyond the books, there was my teacher, Nayla, the regal female jaguar at the Seattle zoo. I was familiar with rushing around the zoo as a class field trip chaperone, but with Tall Tim's encouragement I began to visit weekly for a time of contemplation and retreat with Nayla. On my first three visits, she was nowhere to be seen. I worried that she was hidden away in some cold concrete room—and sedated, maybe. But her absence also spoke to me of the elusiveness of the jaguar, a friend of solitude.

On my fourth visit, I rounded the corner and there the majestic cat lay, resting peacefully. I found a place to sit across from her, on the other side of the thick glass panel—just like the panel in my dream. I watched Nayla and observed the passing crowd. A little girl shouted and slapped the window, her mother urging her on. "Wake up, jaguar!" they barked. People were screaming and snapping photos and jockeying for position.

Nayla casually raised her head, stood up, and sauntered along the window. Amid all the noise, she suddenly looked smaller, more vulnerable. I was overwhelmed. Tears streamed down my face. This powerful and magnificent creature, meant to roam free across vast distances and sustain huge ecosystems, had become more domesticated than a house cat. I cried for Nayla. And I cried for myself. Here, in this season of darkness, I could see the ways in which the *Possession-Control-Mastery* approach to the world had domesticated and sedated me, through my culture, family, education, and religious heritage. I knew that if I wanted to get my heart back, I would need to face these forces and reclaim my own innate wildness.

The Power of Poetry

In 1994, a group of speleologists (they are cave scientists, I just really wanted to use that word) discovered one of the best-preserved prehistoric art sites in a cave in southeastern France. The figurative paintings at Chauvet–Pont d'Arc cave are estimated to be over thirty thousand years old, and include hand stencils, what seems to be a volcano spewing lava, and more than thirteen species of ice age lions, leopards, bears, and hyenas.

Chauvet cave and many of the countless other ancient rock art locations around the world—many of which are chronicled in the stunning Ancient Art Archive account on Instagram—are understood by anthropologists to be places where ancient rite of passage ceremonies were carried out. To mark their passage into adulthood and a new phase of responsibility, initiates went into the darkness.

And what did they do in the darkness?

They used their imaginations.

They told stories.

They painted.

They *created*.

Many thousands of years later I stumbled upon the power of creating in the darkness. As I transitioned into my full self, my "cave art" of choice was poetry. Initially, I held a candle up to the cave walls and read the poems of others. But as the darkness remained, it didn't take long to notice that there were aches, confusion, and longing within me that needed to be expressed. So I started to sketch my own simple poems.

As poet and civil rights activist Audre Lorde observed, poetry has the power to "give name to the nameless so it can be thought." That's what I began to experience. Just like my jaguar apprenticeship, creating poetry reflected back to me what I could not see. It helped me welcome home rejected parts of myself. Creating poetry became a comforting companion amid disorientation and restlessness. It put some shape—not too rigid or overdefined—to the formless and void phase I was in.

I usually wrote in free form. No rules for structures, like a predefined meter, syllable count, or rhyme scheme.

Often, if a poem I read stirred something in me, I would use it as a jumping off point to dig into what I was feeling. One day I was inspired by a snippet from David Whyte's "Winter Grief" that captured the experience of being in a liminal space. As if I was having a conversation with Whyte's poem, I pulled out my notebook and wrote a brief poem for myself, with no plan to share it with anyone (you'll see why, I'm no Shakespeare):

I am indeed in a season of in between
Still close to the things I've left
And who I've been
And what I've believed

Too close to it all
And yet knowing
I am becoming
And searching

For who I will be
The shape of my soul
The contours of my community
The outline of my work

All of this feels too far away
I long to be nearer to what is emerging
Than what has been
But I know no way to accelerate the journey

Occasionally, I would write haiku, a Japanese poetry style made prominent by Basho in the seventeenth century. A haiku includes a first line of five syllables, a middle line of seven, and a final line of five. Five-seven-five. Haiku is often about a specific event and appeals to the senses. For example, I wrote a haiku about another cat encounter I had one night while I was sitting on my front porch:

A visitation
At dusk, guest uninvited
The stray cat appears

But mostly I avoided any poetic constraints, even though they can be creatively helpful. I knew I just needed to let it flow. To create. To make. Unrestricted. No judgment. I let the words bubble up from within and out onto the page.

Poetry doesn't have to be sophisticated. You don't need to be sitting by a fireplace, wearing a cardigan, and smoking a pipe to write poetry. Poetry can be simple. Regardless of how you go about it, creating poetry will cultivate curiosity, awe, and gratitude within you. All of which are sustenance for the dark night of the soul.

In fact, poetry doesn't need to be your preferred form of "cave art." Any form of creative expression can be supportive during your dark night. Compose songs. Make a quilt. Pull out a canvas and splatter paint on it. Create *anything*; just create *something*.

Kurt Vonnegut, author of satirical works like *Slaughterhouse-Five*, once described the power of creating in a letter he wrote in response to an inquiry from a high school class: "Practice any art, music, singing, dancing, acting, drawing, painting, sculpting, poetry, fiction, essays, reportage, no matter how well or badly, not to get money and fame, but to experience becoming, to find out what's inside you, to make your soul grow."

For me, the added benefit of creating something, even a small something, was that it felt really good! It was satisfying to complete mini projects. As I walked through the dark, I couldn't tell if I had traveled an inch or a mile. The act of creating, however, assured me that I was growing. Not the kind of growth that I used to look to in order to determine my worth in the world—the way I approached roles and projects and success, all related to seeking the approving gaze of others. This was a different kind of growth. Not an ascending to higher levels of influence and wealth or achievement, but a descending kind of growth. I was undergoing. I was becoming.

Death Lodge

As the middle of summer approached, I kept writing poems while I sipped on my morning coffee. I made afternoon visits to Nayla at the zoo when I could duck out of work early. These Ritual Practices nourished me as I continued plodding through the darkness. The kids' excitement about not having school for the next couple months combined with the long sunny days brightened my spirits too.

And then one morning at a local park, the universe let me know that the heavy cloud would one day be lifted.

For Father's Day that year, Cherie helped the kids gift me with a session with our friend Vanya who does spiritual accompaniment, like working with dreams and facilitating ritual experiences. In late July, I finally had time to meet up with her. Vanya called me in advance to get more of a sense of the inner work I was doing.

"It sounds like you need a severance ceremony," she said after listening. "Let's meet at the park next Wednesday."

The following week, after dropping the kids off at summer camp, I made my way over to my favorite local park for the ritual. It was a place I knew well, a place I had been to more than a hundred times for family hikes, early morning trail runs, birthday parties, low tide field trips, and family photo shoots. This time, however, I was going for a severance ceremony, though I wasn't exactly sure what that would entail.

I descended into the forested seaside park on a hiking trail and found Vanya waiting in a small clearing in the woods near a stream where salmon run every November. There was a circle on the ground, populated with small objects, including a stone skull and candles. She welcomed me into the circle by surrounding me with smoke from the small bundle of sage that she lit. She then began to explain aspects of the particular severance ceremony I was going to participate in. It was called the *death lodge*.

I first heard of the death lodge concept while reading *Soulcraft*. A death lodge is an actual or imagined place in which a person says goodbye to the identity they have outgrown. The death lodge is about untying yourself from all that has limited you, both positive and negative patterns, so that you can live fully in the present. You bid farewell to your former ways of being and moving through the world, to ways of relating, social identities, organizational affiliations, and family-of-origin roles.

The death lodge is a place where gratitude and grief are intertwined. Gratitude for love, relationships, roles, and change.

Grief for all of the same things, and for personal and collective pain and loss.

In the small clearing at the park, Vanya invited me to reflect on my own gratitude and grief. While there had been mourning in the years leading to that circle and there would be mourning in the months ahead, in that moment I felt a surge of gratitude for all that I was leaving behind. What a gift it was to create and lead a community. How beautiful it was to give my life in service to my vulnerable neighbors, spurred on by faith. I was thankful for my loyalty and dedication, and my strong work ethic and drive, compliments of my parents and generations before them. And despite the dynamics of my work, I was even grateful for the religious affiliations forged in my upbringing and along my vocational path. Because even as I had experienced the restrictive and harmful nature of the church, I had also been a witness of and collaborator with countless ambassadors of love and light in the work of extending belonging, compassion, and justice.

Vanya then explained that all these commitments and endeavors and ways of being—all that I had given myself to—could be represented by the four directions on the circle. North, South, East, and West. She pointed out that while some of my directions were overdeveloped, there were other sections that I had not tended to.

I had dedicated my life to two directions. To the North, a kingly kind of energy marked by leadership, responsibility, and power. And to the East, an energy expressed in community and work. Meanwhile, I had neglected other directions. The ignored, desolate areas described by Vanya correlated exactly with the parts of me that I had been increasingly drawn to: the wildness and play of the South, the transformation and sensuality of the West.

Pointing at the circle, Vanya said, "You know which directions you want to depart from in your life. Now it is time for you to consider these as you go for a wander in the park. Which direction do you want to walk in for your death lodge in order to observe what you are leaving or where you are going?"

I knew what she was asking. I told her that I wanted to go to the northeast part of the park that symbolized where I had spent most of my life, that I needed to go to the North and East for my death lodge as an expression of gratitude for all it gave me, as a confirmation that I had outgrown that life, and as a vow that I would make room for the South and West parts of myself.

She then sent me off with some simple instructions: "Be open to the conversation nature or your soul wants to have with you. You might experience something profound or it might seem ordinary. Whatever happens is what needs to happen. Come back in an hour and tell me your story."

The Owl Encounter

I walked away to the northeast part of the park. My expectations for the next hour were low, but I was thankful for the reflective space and Vanya's accompaniment. And besides, it was a gorgeous summer day for a walk in the woods.

I followed a beam of sunlight piercing through the canopy of trees. It brought me to a stream that led me to a spider that pointed me down a path. After a short walk, I crossed a small bridge—it was a threshold to another realm. I pushed aside some overgrown shrubs and realized that it was a trail I had never been on. I never even knew it existed.

I continued down the path. I felt pulled into a more playful, imaginative state of consciousness. I stared into the deep hollow of a massive moss-covered maple tree. I picked up a walking stick that became a sword. I took off my shirt and swung the sword through the air. I felt like my ten-year-old son.

Then I saw a fallen tree across a shallow ravine. Before I knew it (and without much thought of how falling off and breaking some bones would impact our summer vacation scheduled to start the next day), I was slowly making my way across it. When I reached the other side, I crouched and growled like a jaguar.

It was as if my ignored directions of wildness and sensuality had been activated as soon as I left the circle. It wasn't even noon yet. But that didn't matter. I was in dreamtime.

I got back on the trail and kept walking for a few more minutes. Suddenly, I heard a heavy flutter. I could almost feel the force of it on the back of my head. *That sounds like a big bird,* I thought. I stopped and looked around. I took a few steps off the path through the plants and bushes scratching my ankles. And that's when I saw it. A massive, majestic barred owl perched in a tree thirty yards away, staring right at me.

The owl swooped down toward me, landing twenty yards away, still looking at me. I was stunned into stillness. A minute later it flew toward me once more, landing on a branch less than ten yards away. It looked directly at me and seemed to be peering into my soul.

I slowly raised my arm for the owl to land on it. And the owl . . . did nothing. It stayed right where it was (hey, I figured it was worth a try!). Regardless, I felt absolutely present to what was transpiring. It wasn't a time to process things. And yet, I couldn't help but think:

I've been to this park a hundred times and I've never seen an owl here!

It's 11:30 am on a sunny summer day and here is this nocturnal creature!

I'm at the park exploring themes of death and darkness.

I'm looking for a message, and here in front of me is an owl, which I know at a very basic Harry Potter level is a symbol of a magical realm and a deliverer of messages!

We looked at each other for a long time. I waited for the owl to fly away. But it wouldn't. It was waiting for me to leave. As I turned around to head back to the circle, I sensed that the owl was letting me know that it was watching me and that it was with me in the darkness.

I returned to the circle where Vanya was waiting. Cherie joined us too. I told them the whole story. They were in disbelief, later confessing that at first they thought I was making up the owl part, as if I got the assignment wrong and was using my imagination instead of my actual experience. After I finished speaking, Vanya retold the story of my one-hour *Wander* in the woods back to me. But in her retelling it was an epic adventure. I was facing my fears and befriending the wild. I was tapping into my inner strength and innate wildness. Before she offered a closing blessing she suggested that I occasionally return to where I met the owl. It was my death lodge, a place for grief and gratitude that would help me continue on through this season of death and darkness.

Later on I did some research and found out that owls are messengers of death and symbolize the ability to navigate any darkness in life. Of course that's what owls do! And of course I encountered an owl when I did, in my own season of darkness—a season of severance from my connections to meaningful vocational roles, from my accustomed ways of showing up in family and friendship, from my faith tradition and its structures of belief.

What Happened in the Darkness

My jaguar teacher, the power of poetry, and the death lodge experience sustained me in the darkness. But what really happens in the dark night of the soul? We usually don't find out until later. But David Whyte is on the right track in the poem "Sweet Darkness" where he says darkness is the place where you "give up all the other worlds except the one to which you belong."

We often chase after light in the world. The light, we think, is where we find answers or clarity or guarantees—something steady and certain to attach to. But to descend into the dark depths, or find yourself there, is to refuse to give your allegiance to anyone or anything else but your true self. No system or technique. No construct of God or social pressure. No father or mother or lover. No impostor identity, no mascot costume, no illusion. In the empty darkness, there is only you, the true wellspring of your love and power. And this is the core, essential you that cannot be taken away and cannot be extinguished.

In the darkness, I arrived at the end of myself.

Which was also the beginning of myself.

And it was love.

I just didn't know it yet.

"Come forth into the light of things.
Let nature be your teacher."

**—William Wordsworth,
"The Tables Turned"**

"You enter the forest at the darkest point,
where there is no path. Where there
is a way or path, it is someone else's
path. You are not on your own path. If
you follow someone else's way, you are
not going to realize your potential."

**—Joseph Campbell,
*The Hero's Journey***

5

WANDER IN THE WILD

Walk on the Wild Side

The owl encounter not only affirmed my capacity to endure the darkness, it also amplified what I had been hearing for a number of months, especially when I would visit the domesticated Nayla at the zoo: the call of the wild.

Just like entering the darkness, wandering in the wild also shows up consistently in stories of awakening. In the *Ramayana*, the Sanskrit epic, Rama spends his fourteen years in exile in the forest. Jesus' forty-day identity crisis didn't take place on a laptop at the corner coffee shop. He was fasting in the desert. He also regularly withdrew from the hustle and bustle of daily life for solitude in remote places. A thousand years later, Sufi mystics had a similar extreme desert fasting experience known as the *chelle*, Persian for "forty." Nature is also a central character in the Lakota vision quest. The same is true for the Australian aboriginal walkabout. In fact, ancient rite of passage ceremonies across cultures consistently immerse the initiates in the solitude of the forest, mountainside, desert, or some other fierce landscape. All of these wandering-in-the-wild rituals are about going away from the safety and familiarity of the community, and about embracing vulnerability in the presence of the natural world.

That's because the wild has so much to teach us. Things that we cannot learn from a book or online course or degree program. As an African shamanic healer named Dorcas says in John Neafsey's *A Sacred Voice Is Calling*, "How can you know anything if you don't go out? How can people learn about the spirits of the mountains and the rivers if you just go to the university? No, to learn about the spirits you must go out alone into the wild places."

Similarly, the fundamental premise of the work of Bill Plotkin, whose book *Soulcraft* was my bible during this season, is that nature is a mirror to the human soul. The reason we struggle to know ourselves is because we live in a society largely cut off from the natural world. But when you open up to the wild, you can hear again what you are meant to hear—the voice of God, of the universe, of your soul.

Answering the call of the wild isn't about a frenetic, prankster, *Jackass* kind of wild. Nor does it involve adopting some aggressive, barbaric form of masculinity. It's not about bagging an elk. And it isn't about becoming a wilderness expert like Bear Grylls either (though his survival skills might come in handy!). Embracing wildness has nothing to do with mastering or conquering. It's the opposite of *Possession-Control-Mastery*. It's about submitting to nature. About opening yourself up to the wisdom of wild things.

The Why of Wandering

On the journey to get your heart back, where there is *wild*, there is *wandering* too. In other words, in many stories wandering is often the primary mode of moving through the wild. Moses led Israel through the wilderness for forty nomadic years. Odysseus gets tossed around the sea. Merry and Pippin get lost in Fangorn Forest.

The same goes for anyone who walks this path. As Plotkin observes, "This is precisely the sort of courage and action required of the Wanderer: to sacrifice his [or her] dependence upon old forms and routines derived from other hearts and minds, to learn to rely on a deeper identity."

After you leave home, the old maps—reliable and helpful for so long—no longer work. You must forsake your well-trodden ways of moving through the world. You must also abandon the routine paths that others have put before you. Instead, you must get lost in the unknown. This is what makes way for the renovation of your being. This same impulse is addressed by the practice of pilgrimage, which is a form of wandering. It covers the terrain between the familiar and the fresh, setting the conditions for the fullest expression of who you are to emerge.

Wandering is also an evasion tactic. After you cross the threshold of change, the whole assortment of Impostors you left behind still try desperately to get your attention. Just because there is no turning back for you, it doesn't stop them—or at least their ghosts—from attempting to haunt you and distract you in this next stage of your awakening.

You've got a great career, why would you mess it up by following some so-called mystical experience?

Sure, you got hurt a lot in that relationship, but wasn't it good enough? You don't want to end up alone, do you?

Remember the good ole days, how amazing things were? Wasn't it so much easier and so much better back then, back there?

Embracing the wanderer spirit quiets these voices and enables you to see through the illusory seductions of stability, security, and safety presented by your Impostor.

White Mustang in the Desert

Half a year after the owl encounter, I was driving across the desert for a work trip that would also involve wandering among the wild places of the American Southwest.

Nico was with me. I'd invited him because the meetings were relevant to his role in the organization, but mostly because I really wanted to get some of what he calls "windshield time" with him so we could talk. I also thought he might like to do some desert wandering with me. When I initially asked him, he immediately said yes, before telling me to bring my sleeping bag.

"We're spending a night outside," he stated.

"We are?" I asked. "Where?"

"We'll figure it out," he said confidently.

Apparently he had been feeling the call of the wild too.

The trip felt enchanted from the moment I arrived at the El Paso airport when the rental agent called me "Mister Cat," and then directed me to a complimentary upgrade, a white Mustang convertible. Both were significant omens because I was in the midst of my jaguar apprenticeship, and the horse had become Nico's guide. Getting a convertible was a bonus—even though it was during the cold of January—and it gave the whole adventure a bit of a Thelma and Louise fleeing-across-the-desert vibe.

I had a few meetings that afternoon before I returned to the airport to get Nico. He was ecstatic about the Mustang. We put the top down and drove west out of town under the stars into New Mexico. After a little while, we pulled over to the side of the road to put the roof back up so we wouldn't freeze to death. Our conversation was immediately bouncing all over the place between our kids and college stories, existential questions and updates on our respective marriages, with the occasional freestyle rap mixed in for good measure.

It was exactly what I needed. I had felt a growing need for his *anam cara* presence. For a while, I had been experiencing a lightness of being, an emerging contentment, and a slowly growing creative energy. But then I started to feel the encroachment of some negative energy, like Gollum lurking in the shadows and trailing Frodo through Mordor. Once again, it was my Impostor.

This, it turns out, is to be expected. Passage through the Falling phase is a long and arduous road, filled with many trials. There's always another mountain to climb, another river to cross, another dragon to slay. But I was slow and stubborn when it came to acknowledging this. And it left me worn and weary, which is why I was so thrilled about the hours of drive time I would have with Nico to spill my soul. I needed his support. Unsurprisingly, everything we talked about as we rode across the desert in the white Mustang that first night turned out to be the preparation I needed for the conversation and encounter that I would have with the wild the following day.

The Dad Dream

As we continued along on a road hugging the Mexico border, we sank deeper and deeper into conversation.

"Did I ever tell you about the second dream I had the same night as my jaguar dream six months ago?" I asked.

He thought about it for a moment. "Remind me," he said.

So I told him the dream:

My dad is sitting in a reclining sofa chair with his hand resting on his chest, a posture that is basically a genetic trait in the family line. I start to tell him about how I'm changing and growing. How I'm evolving. But every time I open my mouth, he starts to mock me. After each thing I say, he starts defensively yelling at me, as if the perspective I'm sharing is a direct attack on him. But I'm not even talking about him. I'm talking about me. I'm sad and frustrated. But I also feel strong. No matter what insult he throws at me, I feel undeterred from the direction I am moving in.

"How did it feel?" Nico asked.

Without even having to think about it, I told him that it felt familiar, except for the mocking part. Opinionated and defensive? Yes. But not mocking.

"So what do you think it means?" he wondered.

And began to tell him what I discovered when I worked on the dream with Vanya.

It was my dad in the dream. I knew that for sure.

My dad had left his hometown as soon as he could, leaving the family auto service and repair business and going on to become a successful attorney. From a young age, just as his father had before him, he reinforced the idea with us that working hard and achieving were essential, non-negotiable. My dad generously told me again and again how proud of me he was for my accomplishments in everything and anything I was involved in—academics, sports, music, and even my performance as the Main Brain Vince Fontaine in my high school's production of the musical *Grease*. I witnessed the same thing in how he talked about and treated my three brothers. In a world where so many men long for this kind of praise from their fathers and never receive it, this was an incredible gift!

And yet it also came at a cost. A part of me internalized my dad's expression of pride as meaning *I am loved for what I do*. I learned to associate my worth with what I achieved. And so I did more and more to try to earn acceptance from my parents and the people around me. I learned to bury any uncomfortable feelings so I could focus on the work in front of me, to "get over it" so I could tend to the task at hand. This is how the Impostor, with its obsessions with producing and perfecting, became such a powerful force in me.

It made sense that my dad was showing up in my dream. Because, without a doubt, what I was doing—letting go of this mask and choosing to no longer let my life revolve around work and achievement—was a direct challenge to his way of moving through the world. It was a refutation of much of what I had picked up from him about who I am. The dream was a symbol of my own necessary inner confrontation with the *I-am-what-I-do* story. But I wondered if it would also require a confrontation with my dad in the waking world.

It absolutely was my dad in the dream, I said again to Nico.

But, I added, *it was also more than my dad.*

This image of my dad was an archetype too, a recurring

symbol in human consciousness that surfaces in dreams and myths, as Vanya had explained to me. More specifically, it was the *King* archetype. My dad in his recliner was actually a King on his throne. A representation of power and authority. But it wasn't a healthy King who brings order, blessing, and inspiration. It was a distorted version—a *Tyrant King* who tries to control and diminish others. A Darth Vader kind of character. The image of my dad represented the external pressure to conform and fit in, an especially strong force in my church background, but also pervasive throughout the *Possession-Control-Mastery* society that wants to keep everyone on the hamster wheel of producing and consuming.

The Tyrant King archetype was a signal to me that crossing the threshold is never a neutral activity. The resistance and opposition present in the Leaving phase continue into the Falling phase. There are always voices telling us to follow the rules, stay small, stick with what we've always known, and believe what we've always believed.

It was my dad in the dream.

It was this Tyrant King force too.

But that wasn't it, I explained to Nico. *It was also me.*

We show up in our own dreams as multiple different characters. A part of me was sitting in that chair too. It was a distorted version of the part of me that had done good work and been responsible and cared for others well. It was a malformed version of this *North* part of me, where I had spent so much of my life, as I had acknowledged that day in the circle with Vanya before encountering the owl in the woods. This Tyrant King *within me* was trying to intimidate and silence the emerging true and wild parts of me instead of blessing them. This inner Tyrant King was mocking me because it didn't want me to leave what had been a pretty good setup. After all, it worked for a long time, didn't it? It was trying to scare me away from the unknown that comes with growing. *Don't shed. Don't put yourself out there. Don't change. Don't be vulnerable. Stay here. Just play it safe.*

I finished explaining the multiple meanings of the dream to Nico and there was a long silence.

"That's some serious shit," he responded as we drove past the first of many intimidating border patrol vehicles we would see lurking in the darkness that night.

Reverent, Obedient Cadet

A little while later I asked, "Were you ever a part of Cadets as a kid?" I was referring to our church denomination's version of Boy Scouts (but without all the survival skills).

"I totally was!" he said, laughing.

"Remember the pledge?" I continued. "A cadet must be reverent, obedient, compassionate, consecrated, trustworthy, pure, grateful, loyal, industrious, and cheerful."

Nico spontaneously joined me in reciting the words. He knew them too.

"There's actually some good stuff in there," he observed. "Why do you bring it up?"

"Because of the whole 'reverent, obedient' part," I explained. These words captured the pressure I experienced as a kid— and even into adulthood in the religious context in which I worked—to stay in line in order to fit in. To conform to the expectations of others in order to be accepted. To always have my shit together. To be a good boy.

"So you don't upset the Tyrant King in your dream, right?" Nico reflected. "It reminds me of what Bill Plotkin calls the 'loyal soldier,'" he added. "It's a part of you that has fulfilled its role trying to protect you. But the war is over, so the loyal soldier's service is no longer needed."

"Exactly," I replied, "For a while my inner reverent, obedient cadet kept me safe from being judged and cast out by my community. But over time it forced me to shut down my inner wildness and other parts of myself. It turned against me."

Shedding my perfectionist, achievement-oriented Impostor helped me discover the *reverent, obedient cadet* mask beneath it. The mask behind the mask. It was my most dominating Impostor, I explained.

Nico answered, "Sounds like you need to have another talk with your inner reverent, obedient cadet and tell him his work is done, Mister Cat-man."

"Yeah, I think you're right," I affirmed.

Then he added, "And maybe it's time to have a talk with your dad too."

The sacred conversation lasted for six hours as we rode the white Mustang across the desert under the sparkling stars. It was a *thin space,* as the Celtic tradition says, when the veil between earth and heaven seems transparent. Omens seemed to be everywhere as cats and horses showed up in business and school signs, and the names of streets and towns. At one point, a jackrabbit darted out in front of the car. I didn't have time to stop or swerve. We got out of the car and held a brief funeral.

As Nico and I crouched beside the deceased creature, it was no longer roadkill; it was our teacher. Reminding us of our own mortality—of the spiritual deaths we were in the midst of and of our eventual deaths. *This is our common destination*, I thought. *What else is there to do than to live fully and love fiercely here and now?*

While our means of wandering would shift from driving to walking the next day, the wild desert had already begun enveloping us. It was working on me, surfacing the themes that I needed to address. Sometime after midnight, a couple hours after we entered Arizona, we drove up a mountainside road in the Coronado National Forest, found a place to sleep, and rolled out our sleeping bags under the stars.

Spots of Time

Many months earlier, shortly after my jaguar dream session with Tall Tim, eager to enact my dream image of leaving the dilapidated house for the wild jungle, I signed up for a two-week wilderness quest. But I would have to wait almost a year for it. Meanwhile, my desire to be in the wild was only increasing, especially after the owl encounter. And so, in the months leading up to the road trip with Nico, I embraced a variety of Ritual Practices that facilitated my conversation with the natural world.

My family explored new hiking spots. As an excuse to get lost even deeper in the woods, I picked up trail running and ended up running a few marathons. When my fall travel schedule for work got busy, I planned meetings and transitions and flight times so I could wander in the wild as much as possible.

In one spiritual direction session, I said to Tall Tim, *I want to travel in spirit, to talk to spirit, to hear spirit.* He said it seemed like each work trip was a "mini quest." I liked how that sounded. So I approached each trip with openness and curiosity, whether I was wandering by an alligator-filled swamp in Florida or along the rushing river of a Colorado canyon, in southern California's low desert or on a snowy rural road in Canada.

My work took me to faraway places, but when it comes to wandering in the wild, you don't have to travel around the world to converse with nature. This is important: Do not mistake the outer journey for the inner journey. Many people get distracted by the idea of traveling great distances and visiting exotic locales as the way to unleash the wild self, but these can just as easily be forms of escape and avoidance.

I had the travel and trail runs, but mostly I immersed myself in the wild by visiting a place not too far from my house—that spot just across the small wooden bridge, past where I swung a stick in the air like a young boy, and beyond where I crossed the fallen log like a prowling jaguar—the spot in the woods where I met the owl during my death lodge.

It became my *spot of time.*

Spots of time, the English Romantic poet William Wordsworth wrote, are places with "a renovating virtue" that nourish and repair our minds. Places that offer solace, where you experience a kind of mystical communion with nature.

Not only are these places in nature restorative, they are also instructive. As theologian Belden Lane writes in *The Great Conversation,* "The world is full of teachers ready to carry us into amazement." His *spot of time* was at the city park just across the street where he developed a sacred friendship over twenty-five years with a single cottonwood tree he called "Grandfather."

Spots of time are everywhere. The vines growing on your fence. Your dog's favorite tree down the block. The edge of the local baseball diamond outfield. We are in a wild world—and *we are the wild world*—every day. What is lacking is our attention. Our brains are so skilled at identifying patterns that we easily cling to identifying something as a tree, mushroom, or squirrel, rather than bringing mindful awareness to the unique and magical thing we are in the presence of. When we embrace this kind of contemplative approach, and add a dash of childlikeness, we soon find ourselves receiving or hearing from the plant, animal, or landscape in front of us. We are invited into a deeper story.

I first heard the phrase *spot of time* while listening to a podcast during a trail run at the exact moment I arrived at the owl tree one day. Not even a minute later, the same owl returned, this time perching on a distant tree branch and staring at me. I never saw the owl again—though I did encounter a coyote, salmon, woodpeckers, bald eagles, and countless slugs in the surrounding area—but I kept coming back to that subtle bend on the path as much as I could. When I was confused and lost, I could return there and find myself again. The spot lifted me up when I needed it. It was a place to cry. To celebrate. To complain. To be grateful. Because of that sacred space, even as I was Falling into the unknown, my frustrations with my career and anxieties about the future faded away. I began to see everything as an opportunity to grow, to practice presence, to extend love and care to whoever was in front of me.

Even now, as I live across the country, it remains my *spot of time* that I return to when I'm in town. I've returned in the summer heat and the chilly winter rain, at dawn and at dusk. No matter when I go or what I'm going through—confusions with my calling, frustrations with family or friends, anxiety or fear—this wild place always gives me a little piece of my heart back. That's what *spots of time* do.

The Art of the Wild Wander

Our conversation with the wild can center on these places we come to know intimately, like my place in the woods. But it can also be carried on with places we spontaneously discover in a moment, like the area Nico and I visited the day after our late-night drive along the border. That morning we woke up and found a roadside diner where we ordered eggs, bacon, and coffee to warm us. Our plan was to do a daylong *Wander.*

A Wander is an intentional time in the wild to connect with soul, God, and nature. The practice of the wander welcomes all body types, whether in a remote, rugged place or in a more accessible place like a neighborhood park. Just like visiting a *spot of time,* this is a more engaged way of being with nature. Not an aggressive hike or mountain peak summit or attempt to set a daily step record. A Wander is slow and still.

A Wander is an energetic dialogue with a place. It is similar to the Japanese practice of *shinrin-yoku,* or forest bathing—a type of ecotherapy that brings healing by fostering connection with the natural world. The Wander, however, may invite a walk in the woods (or other landscape) that is a bit more lively.

Belden Lane retells a Hasidic Jewish story that captures the power of the Wander practice. Every day, instead of attending morning prayers in the synagogue, a boy wandered alone in the woods. His father was concerned for his safety and said, "I'm glad you are searching for God, but you don't have to go out to the woods. God is the same everywhere!" "Yes," the boy responded, "but I'm not." As Lane observes, "God might be the same everywhere, but [the boy] knew there was something different about *him* out in the wilds. Stripped of things familiar, he was more vulnerable, more open and receptive."

The primary consideration for a day Wander is *safety*. Tell someone where you're going. Get a map and know your way around. Wear proper attire. Bring food and water.

The next concern is *ritual*. There are many design considerations that can aid you in your descent into the underworld realm of the Wander. First, set an *intention* for your time. Will you be engaging your grief, gratitude, death, or confusion? Something else? Second, identify a *threshold* to cross as you begin. A stream, a stone, a trail sign. The threshold sets apart the Wander experience as sacred. It helps you enter into the magic of dreamtime. Third, just as I did the day I was led to the owl, *be a follower*. Follow the light shining through the leaves. Follow the birdsong. Follow the shape of a cloud. These practices might take you on a long, meandering trek through the forest, or deliver you to the trunk of a tree that you need to sit with for a few hours. Following will take you exactly where you need to be.

If These Rocks Could Talk

As we ate our breakfast, Nico and I scoured Google Maps on our phones to figure out where to go for our Wander. Abruptly, he got up from the table and walked outside. Through the window I saw him approach an old man and start talking. Then the man pointed at the mountains in the distance. A minute later Nico returned and explained, "I saw that guy's shirt. It had a pointing skeleton on it, so I felt like I needed to ask him for directions about where we should go for the day."

"Well, what did he say?" I asked, amazed.

"We need to go toward Brown Canyon in the Miller Peak Wilderness Area."

So that's where we went.

We let our families know where we were going and agreed to meet each other back at the car six hours later. Then we parted ways. As I took my first steps on the trail, it hit me that I was now on a quest within a quest within a quest—at a life level, a road trip level, and a day Wander level. Soon a buzzing bee greeted me and was my first escort. Next it was a swarm of flies. They carried me up and out of a steep green canyon and then down into a dark forest. Eventually, I was pulled off the trail to a small clearing where four stones, arranged naturally around an invisible circle, set the scene for a confrontation with my false self—the conversation with my reverent, obedient cadet that Nico had predicted the night before.

I sat on the *North* rock, the direction representing power, authority, and responsibility—my inner King. This was the space I had occupied most of my life. In my imagination, I sat there as a diminished, immature version of the King, as one who had let the Tyrant King bully him into submission—the reverent, obedient cadet, my final Impostor. This was the space I had occupied most of my life. On that rock, a host of avoided feelings rose to the surface. My bitter discontent, fueled by comparison. My jealousy, burning at the wealth and success and career choices of friends, who on the surface all seemed so sure, so secure, so stable. My rage at the restrictive roles of religion and whiteness in my life and all the destruction caused by *Possession-Control-Mastery* in the world. Heat filled my body and rose up to my head.

I stared across at the *South* stone—the wild stone, so small and underdeveloped. A neglected part of me.

"Forgive me," I said. It was a simple statement, but it held so much.

It was an apology for all the compliance.

For hiding preferences and opinions.

For pretending to fit into a religious system and other spaces out of fear of rejection.

For insisting that I act modest and proper.

For working so hard to be inoffensive.

For staying small and wanting everyone to like me.

For trying to grow up so fast and taking on so much responsibility because I thought I had it all together.

For moving with such intense drive from one thing to the next.

There was more too, I'm sure.

I waited for a response.

Come over here, I sensed my wild self whispering from the *South* stone. So I went and sat down, looking back to the *North* rock where I had just been. *It wasn't for nothing,* my wild self added. *Look.*

And when I looked at the *North* rock, I saw the frail cadet. But I could also see how even in an immature form, it was an expression of my inner King. A radiant power. Not controlling, but loving and serving. I saw countless lives transformed and people cared for by my reverence and obedience, by my leadership and responsibility and drive. I saw the woman I love and our stunning children, all results of my eagerness to grow up so fast. I saw my friends, heard our hearty laughter, and felt their loving presence. I saw an old soul, seasoned from so many years of spiritual seeking, spurred on by the deep wells of religious wisdom I had been exposed to and by the loving spiritual communities and the awakened individuals within them that supported me.

"Thank you," I said out loud to a random, unremarkable rock in the woods that was at the same time a part of me. The part of me that had done the only thing it knew how to do given my upbringing and identities and social pressures.

And then, in what was yet another expression of leaving and letting go on this journey of getting my heart back, I retired my last Impostor, my reverent, obedient cadet: "You have served me well. But I can't go any further on the path to wholeness with you. It's over. Your work here is done." Uttering these words while sitting on the south stone was to claim both my wild and my royal natures. It was an affirmation that both belonged.

The Owl's Club

A couple hours later Nico and I reunited back at the white Mustang. We drove on to Tucson. That night we traded stories of our respective Wanders over dinner. I told him about my experience with the circle of stones, and about a secret name I received afterward. And he recounted his journey to the foot of a knotted tree, the shadow of a cliff, and the interior of a muddy cave. When we finished, I asked the waiter for a bar recommendation for a post-dinner cocktail.

"Owl's Club," he said without hesitation. Nico chuckled. He knew what the owl meant to me. The waiter added, "It's an old funeral parlor that turned into a bar."

Of course it was. I was just looking for a cocktail, but what I got was a reminder that I was on the right path, and foreshadowing of the theme of the wilderness quest I would embark on a few months later when I descended into a mysterious canyon.

Nico and I continued swapping stories at the Owl's Club over Old Fashioned cocktails while an anxious, aging performer dressed in a camel-colored suit and a cowboy hat played some country tunes. The next morning I had a few more meetings before leaving for Phoenix. On the way, we pulled off the highway and parted ways for another Wander. This time I ended up having an intimate experience with a saguaro cactus that left me naked and weeping. I returned home the following day, my heart a bit more restored by the generosity and kindness of the wild.

Houston, We No Longer Have a Problem

One month later I was sitting at another bar. This time in Houston. And I was having another critical conversation, one foreshadowed by Nico. But it wasn't with a symbolic circle of stones. It was with my dad.

Earlier I had finished a dinner meeting, and when I checked my texts I noticed my dad was commenting on downtown Houston in a family text thread. *That's random. He doesn't even know I'm here,* I thought. And then it dawned on me that he might also be in Houston.

"Are you in Houston?" I texted.

"Yep," he replied, "Here for depositions. At a bar downtown."

I couldn't believe it. *My quest continues,* I thought.

"I'm in downtown Houston too!" I quickly texted back.

Ten minutes and a two-mile drive later, I was sitting with my dad, both of us in awe of the chance encounter. We hadn't seen each other in more than six months, so I was just grateful to be with him. I didn't have any agenda to open up about the deeper aspects of my life. He started asking me questions about my job. He knew I was dissatisfied and I said as much. But then he kept inquiring.

"How are you?" he asked. "The last few times I've seen you, you haven't seemed well. I've been worried about you."

It felt like a gentle invitation. So I opened up about the journey I was on. Not all of the crazy stories, but the essence of it. Getting too wrapped up in what I do and achieve. Learning a new way to be in the world. Changes in what I believe and don't believe, and questioning the importance of belief itself.

He was concerned, asking a whole bunch of questions about church, the Bible, and theology. He was direct, like any good lawyer, but he was also genuinely curious—the exact opposite of the Dad-King-Impostor character from the dream I had. Unlike previous interactions we'd had around these themes, I felt safe and seen. Not an ounce of anxiousness or fear about what he might think. Fully present in myself. No desire to convince him of anything. No pressure to pretend.

In other words, my reverent, obedient cadet was nowhere to be found. Thanks to wandering in the wild, I was free.

It felt like two friends listening and learning from one another. To anyone else in the bar, it looked like a normal conversation, but for me it was a holy moment, years in the making. As the bar closed, we walked outside and hugged. He kissed me on the cheek. He told me how special our conversation was. And he told me how much he loved me.

I was able to receive the love. From him, of course. But also from myself, from the divine, from everything. A love not based on any accomplishment or behavior or belief. An unconditional love.

The Wind Whispers My Name

Earlier, during the day Wander, at the exact moment I had concluded my ceremony in the circle of stones, a strong wind swept through the trees and a thick hush filled the canyon. A family of birds appeared, and soon I was following them, like the bee and swarms of flies that had initiated my Wander hours earlier. The birds bounced from branch to branch and sent me up a switchback trail.

As I approached the summit, I felt beckoned off of the trail. I climbed over a field of boulders until I arrived at a rocky perch high above the circle of stones below and across from a massive green canyon wall. As the wind swirled around me, I inched closer to the edge of the cliff. I felt rooted and strong, aware of my patience and endurance. I was grateful and open-hearted from my experience in the circle of stones. I wasn't asking for anything more. I stood still.

Then I heard a name, whispered by the wind.

It was a name for me—a new name, but also a name I always had. A name I was always searching for. The name spoke of who I was becoming on this journey to get my heart back. It spoke of who I had become now that I had released my reverent, obedient cadet in the canyon below. It spoke of who I have always truly been.

I received the sacred name.

Then, slowly, I raised my arms. I caught the wind in my hands. And with a full-throated roar I spoke back my new and ancient name.

To the wind.

To all the wild things.

And also to the wandering, the act that was freeing me from conformity, enabling me to access my grief and gratitude, and healing me.

"For whoever wants to save their life will lose it, but whoever loses their life for me will find it."

—Matthew 16:25

"And where we had thought to find an abomination, we shall find a god; where we had thought to slay another, we shall slay ourselves; where we had thought to travel outward, we shall come to the center of our own existence, where we had thought to be alone, we shall be with all the world."

—Joseph Campbell,
The Hero with a Thousand Faces

6

FACE YOUR DEATH

The Bones Are Good

A few months after facing my father, I was all by myself setting up camp for three days of solitude in a deserted canyon in southern Utah. After doing group work for a week at a retreat center and wilderness base camp, it was my first day alone on the quest I had been anticipating since my jaguar dream a year earlier.

The campsite for my "solo" experience was located in the perfect place. I had chosen this spot the previous day when we were sent out in pairs to find our respective areas for solitude and fasting. I was grateful that my partner for the search was Dr. Neil since I felt most connected to him on the quest. We wandered out from the group base camp for a few miles and crossed a few small streams before ascending along a dried-up creek bed. As we came around a slight bend, I looked to the left and saw a shimmering light coming through a grove of ponderosa pine trees. I had no idea what would transpire in that particular place a few nights later, but I instantly heard it calling me. My invitation to that grove was confirmed a moment later when Dr. Neil crouched down by some small shrubs and picked up a bone.

"Holy shit, it's a shoulder blade," he exclaimed.

Slightly nervous and looking for reassurance, I asked, "You mean an *animal's* shoulder blade, right?"

The doctor hesitated, and then answered with the subtle sound of a question in his voice, "I think so."

After surveying the land a bit more, we discovered more bones violently scattered around. Thankfully, they belonged to a deer or a goat, not a human. The presence of the bones was another omen, fitting the consistent theme of the first week of my wilderness quest experience up to that point: *death*. Since my arrival, I had been encountering dead animals. Two chicks, far away from their nest, guarding my entrance to a canyon trail. A small black bird directly outside of the window of my room at the retreat center where we had spent our first few nights. And a bloated fish floating in the creek that I found while I was naked and painted in mud, during a Wander meant to woo my inner wild man. Now I was setting up camp in a den where a cougar had devoured a canyon creature. It was a place of bones and blood, dirt and death. It was exactly where I needed to be.

Death Is the Doorway

The wilderness quest, as noted earlier, encapsulates the *Leaving, Falling, Rising* pattern. But the pinnacle of this rite of passage is death—enacting a spiritual death before one's eventual physical death. This is the ultimate encounter with the self, with the soul. It is at once the end and the beginning. In other words, there is no rising, no return, no renewal, no rebirth without death first. Facing death is the doorway to a more beautiful, full-hearted life.

The old stories speak to this. For example, Jesus is crucified and buried before rising from the dead on the third day. And the Norse god Odin sacrificed himself on Yggdrasil, the world tree, where he hung for nine days and nights with a spear-pierced side until, on the brink of death, he received a revelation. As author Neil Gaiman retells it in *Norse Mythology*, "[Odin] was cold, in agony, and on the point of death when his sacrifice bore dark fruit: in the ecstasy of his agony he looked down, and the runes were revealed to him. He knew them, and understood their power. The rope broke then, and he fell, screaming, from the tree. Now he understood magic. Now the world was his to control."

Modern movie myths repeat this pattern again and again. It's the climactic, all-in-one moment where the protagonist, on the brink of total annihilation, stares death in the face and attains victory over the enemy. Like when the formerly self-absorbed Tony Stark gives up his life, fulfilling Doctor Strange's prediction of the one and only way to defeat evil Thanos and rescue half of the universe.

The same goes for finding your way home. Death is the final foe to face. Transformation cannot transpire without an ego death, the death of who you thought you were. Sometimes this internal, spiritual death you've undergone gets represented by a surprising external experience—a wild encounter, therapeutic discovery, or mystical vision. At other times your spiritual confrontation with mortality may be accompanied by a sudden physical challenge, such an illness or injury. But whether or not anything occurs spontaneously, it is also powerful to intentionally mark your ego death by designing your own rite of passage, such as a pilgrimage, a wander, or a wilderness quest.

Capstone Quest

As Tall Tim had assured me Yoda-style, *on a soul quest, I already was*. And there was no doubt that the journey I was on had been generous to me, providing countless soulful experiences, including multiple opportunities to face my death—dreaming of the jaguar's departure from the decaying house, meeting the owl in the woods during the death lodge ceremony, and discharging my reverent, obedient cadet at the circle of stones. Consequently, I had low expectations for adding any more profound and insightful mystical experiences to my portfolio by participating in a wilderness quest.

Still, I was eager for the unique ways this actual wilderness quest would allow me to exaggerate my demise. Fasting. Solitude. Various Ritual Practices that would help me face my present spiritual death as well as my eventual physical death. And, especially, the opportunity to get off the grid and be cut off from my family, friends, and society. I was ready to push myself to the edge and make myself vulnerable so I could hear whatever I still needed to hear and learn whatever I still needed to learn.

With all of this swirling in my mind as I approached my wilderness quest that spring, I began to think of it as my *capstone* in two senses.

First, it felt like a capstone project, the final requirement of a graduate degree program. But instead of an academic project, my program was soul initiation. The quest marked the completion of a rigorous phase of my life, extending back almost five years. I had already done the bulk of the work. This time alone in the wilderness was more about closure.

Second, it was also my capstone in the original, moribund sense—a large, flat stone forming a roof over the chamber of a megalithic tomb. I was going into the wild, equipped with a shovel and some ceremonies, to bury that former version of myself—reverent and respectable, liked and admired, successful and productive—once and for all.

I knew that my hopes for this quality of experience were not unfounded. Because when I excitedly told my quest plans to an acquaintance who had previously participated in one, he didn't respond with enthusiasm. Instead, he got a somber look on his face and said, "My condolences."

His words would soon make complete sense to me as I sat in starving solitude, beneath the ponderosa pines, for three days, after Dr. Neil found the scattered bones there. But already a few months before the quest began, I experienced a confirmation of his sentiment as the wild prepared me for the deep sorrow that accompanies death.

Saguaro Sorrow

In the desert, just off a highway, down a long dirt road. In the middle of nowhere. It was the day after the Wander in Arizona when I sat in the circle of stones and received a secret name a few months before my quest. An hour earlier Nico and I had parked the car for one last session in the desert before the end of the trip.

I wandered up a small, trailless mountain. A butterfly

greeted me when I arrived at the top and ushered me to the foot of a large saguaro cactus. It was tall, probably over one hundred years old, with four arms clustered together. Suddenly, the cactus spoke to me: "I have a story to tell you."

So I did what anyone would do when a cactus tells you they have a story to tell you. I gave it my full attention. That's when I noticed a two-foot wooden stake plunged through one of the saguaro's arms. I grabbed it and tried to pull it out. It wouldn't budge. The cactus had grown firmly around it.

An image flashed in my mind: Years earlier, someone had hiked up this trailless mountain in the middle of nowhere. That person carried (or found) a wooden stake. Arriving at this particular cactus, in the exact place I now stood, they viciously stabbed the saguaro.

I felt a pang in my side. Then I gasped, overcome with awe. Because the exact thing that the cactus-that-the-butterfly-brought-me-to had said would happen *was actually happening*. It had said it had a story to tell me. And by drawing my awareness to the stake, that's exactly what it was doing. Perhaps sensing my growing belief and how fleeting it might be, the cactus interrupted my excitement with an instruction: "Take off your clothes."

Excuse me. What? Take off my clothes? I must be making this up. I was confused. But I remembered there is precedent for this kind of thing. A burning desert bush once said to a man named Moses, "Take off your sandals, for you are standing on holy ground." Maybe, thousands of years later, this saguaro was essentially saying the same thing. I just had to take off a little more. Maybe the cactus was testing my own willingness to be vulnerable before sharing more of its story.

So in a moment that may or may not be chronicled in some

religion's holy book someday, I took off my shoes. I took off my shirt, my pants, my underwear. I took off everything. And I stood naked in front of a cactus I had just met.

On one hand, because I had been practicing being open and *not* filtering and *not* resisting for so long, I was ready to receive this moment. It was happening. It was real. But on the other hand, even as I was attempting to fully absorb the possibilities of this mystical moment, there was another part of me simultaneously saying, *Hell no, this is not happening right now! Can I just put my pants back on?*

My mind was bouncing back and forth between these two possibilities when, out of the corner of my eye, ten yards from the cactus, I noticed something shiny. Hoping to avoid any sharp pebbles or prickly cholla cactus spines, I carefully stepped toward the metallic object and picked it up. It was a 9mm bullet shell. I turned around to look at the cactus and that's when I noticed for the first time—not only had the cactus been stabbed with the wooden stake, it was also riddled with bullet holes. The desert air suddenly felt thick and heavy. My heart sank.

"See. I told you I have a story to tell you," the cactus whispered before urging me to keep looking.

What transpired in the next ten minutes was part spiritual encounter, part crime scene investigation. I found a second bullet, this one a .38 Special from a different gun, in a patch of grass. Then a third bullet, once again a 9mm, under a small shrub. When I found the fourth bullet, of yet another caliber from another gun, tears started to spill down my face.

With each new discovery, the cactus told me another painful chapter of its story. I was overwhelmed by the amount of violence this cactus had endured. How many people had wandered up this remote, trailless little mountain in the middle of nowhere to take out their rage or sadness or pain on this cactus? But my deep sorrow went beyond the story of this abused cactus. It was as if I was tapping into all the harm throughout the ages that human beings have directed toward every living thing. Toward the planet. Toward one another.

I saw humans, especially men—angry, afraid, confused, sad, lonely, bored men; men suffering under the weight of *Possession-Control-Mastery*—throughout history, lined up to attack this cactus, or another one, or something or someone. Like me, they were far from their true selves. There was a hollowness to their lives. But, somewhere within, there was also a longing for a new story, for a new identity. They just didn't know where to begin. They didn't know if they could summon the courage to go on the journey. And so they settled for a smaller version of themselves. They distracted themselves. They blamed someone or something else. They covered their sadness with rage. They stabbed and shot a cactus.

In that remote place, as the sun was setting, I wept for the cactus and for the entire planet, for myself and for every human being. It was a revelation: All of the struggle and despair and longing that I had experienced, all of the twists and turns on the quest to get my heart back—it had never been just about me. It was always about the bigger story that I belong to, that we all belong to. What brought me to the foot of that cactus wasn't just a personal journey. It was a collective, cosmic journey. I was experiencing what Francis Weller describes in *The Wild Edge of Sorrow*. That our grief is not always personal. It doesn't just result from our life experiences. It's bigger than that, flowing from a deeper, wider expanse.

While it doesn't have to involve a naked encounter with a cactus, touching upon this expanse of sorrow is an inevitable part of the journey home. This is grief work, and there is no way around it. When we begin to acknowledge our personal pain, refusing to dismiss it or cover it up any longer, we come into contact with pain at a planetary level. To tend to our wounds through the expression of grief is to participate in healing the wounds of the world.

Five years earlier on that morning run, it was the divine or the universe telling me *If you don't have your heart, you have nothing.* But it was also grief. Grief interrupted me. A collective sorrow—far heavier than the sadness resulting from any particular incident or story in my privileged life. This deep sorrow was inviting me into healing and wholeness, not just for myself, but for all things, by grieving and tending to my own fragmentation. This is why the journey had been so exhausting, and why my yearning had been so intense. It was always bigger than me.

My pursuit of productivity and perfection had kept my senses numb and ignorant of the reality of pain, loss, and death. But in my quest for renewal, as I experienced disorientation in the darkness and wandering in the wild, the gates of grief began to open wide. And the more I welcomed sorrow, both personal and collective, the more I was prepared to face that I was dying, that I was dead and would die. Because to feel the full weight of grief is also to face death.

This experience with the saguaro, like everything that had happened since my Call to Adventure, was preparing me for the central task of my wilderness quest: my fullest encounter with death.

Descending into Death

A few months later, during the two weeks leading up to my departure, I took care of my final preparations. The wilderness guides had instructed us, with the idea of approaching death in mind, to get our affairs in order. This could involve expressing love or appreciation to someone. Or maybe you need to forgive someone or ask for forgiveness. Perhaps there is an unresolved issue related to your previous life that you need to address. And there are also practical matters. I cleaned up online accounts and passwords. I double-checked my will. I completed some unfinished home improvement projects, which felt like death in and of themselves to this non-handy man. And for some reason, my wife took out a massive life insurance policy on me—kidding!

The guides also gave us strict packing instructions. This quest involved a lot more REI outdoor gear than the original Indigenous practice, I was certain. I combed over the list multiple times to make sure I had everything. No tent, just a tarp. A bunch of layers, smart wool recommended. Some snacks and meals for the non-fasting portion of the trip, and specific water filtration and storage equipment. Also, a biodegradable item to burn in a "fire ceremony." We were also encouraged to bring ceremonial items, clothing or otherwise, for the so-called "trance dance" that was planned. These ceremonial items, the idea was, would help us channel our energies from previous mystical encounters or other sacred moments in our lives. They would draw out our childlike, playful, and open qualities.

So I did what anyone in my situation would do. I went on

Amazon and ordered a jaguar sarong. When it arrived in the mail, I was pretty sure that it was a cheetah print, but nevertheless, I pictured myself in the trance dance in the warm desert air, under the stars, gyrating my hips to a primal drumbeat, half-naked, wearing only my sarong. In reality, however, it was cold in the canyon—so cold that it snowed, and a layer of ice formed on my tarp overnight a few times—and so when it was time for the trance dance, we were mostly just stumbling around in our snow pants. Except for the lovely guy who outdid everyone and hauled a full eagle mascot costume, wings included, into the remote canyon. Even still, I'm sure the gods were swayed by our ceremonial garb.

On my last night before heading off the grid, Cherie and the kids circled around me on the couch. The kids placed their small hands on my shoulders and head and prayed for me. That I would hear from the divine. That I wouldn't get eaten by a mountain lion. Evie, my oldest, affirmed the fact that I was taking time for myself, "even though I'm a dad." Their sweet words washed over me. A powerful benediction, motivating me to fully absorb the experience. And reminding me of how the love of my family had been carrying me this whole time, through the darkness, through the wilderness, through this entire middle passage of the journey.

The next afternoon, after two flights, I arrived at the small retreat center where our quest group consisting of total strangers would spend three days, followed by our descent into the canyon for a few more days of inner work together, before the solo quest. "There are two potential fears people have when entering this kind of experience," our guide Knight said to us, "That *nothing* will happen or that *something* will happen."

Five years earlier, when it all began with *If you don't have your heart, you have nothing*, I likely would have felt these fears too. But after years of pursuing my soul, I had grown familiar with both the silence and the surprises that soul delivers. I was totally open. If nothing happened in that canyon, it was fine. Mystery had already given me so much. But if something did happen, I was ready to receive, ready for revelation, ready to be drawn into the depths of mystery and wonder, into the dark corners of truth and beauty. All over again.

It was a gift to be in the canyon with others who were ready to receive too. As Dr. Neil and I got to know each other, we frequently articulated our readiness to surrender to whatever might unfold by saying to one another, "I'm all in."

Burning the Collar

The night before I set up my campsite and began my solo experience, just a few hours after Dr. Neil had discovered the first of the scattered bones, we all left base camp and crossed over a stream to a small, sandy clearing. We were only twelve hours into our fast, having shared our last meal that morning, but many of us were already feeling hungry. Even more of us were anxious—early the next day we would all go our separate ways, and our solitude would begin. But first it was time for the fire ceremony.

A fire ceremony symbolizes destruction and ending. It can also be a declaration of a new beginning. Whether it's in the wild (in a place with no burn ban!), around a backyard fire pit, or at a living room hearth, it marks moving beyond the Impostor's ways, which keep us small and safe, and venturing forward into wild wholeness.

The pre-quest instructions had told us to bring a symbolic object, representative of something we were leaving behind, to offer up to the sacred flames. Right away I had known that I needed to bring my clerical collar. In my decade as a minister I never actually wore the white priestly collar that often accompanies a black button-up shirt or robe of some sort. It wasn't a part of my church tradition. But it still carried meaning for me. Even beyond the church, people often recognize the collar as a symbol demarcating religious leadership. A minister protesting against some injustice wears a collar to express solidarity with the oppressed. Or a hospital chaplain wears a collar to clearly identify herself as she offers comfort and care up and down the corridors of the oncology center. The clerical collar can be a beautiful symbol. But it can also represent things like institutional control and conformity, hiding behind religiosity, the demand for perfection, and exclusion. Many of the pressures and affiliations I had been shedding for years, and more.

The group sat in silence in a circle, huddled around the dancing flames. We took turns speaking to the fire, the mystery, the object, or God. When it was my turn, I pulled out my collar—it was actually just a thin circular strip of white paper that I had brought so as not to pollute the fresh canyon air with burning the plastic of the real collar. Besides, that meant it weighed next to nothing in my already heavy backpack. Then, in a very undramatic moment, I tossed this simple symbol of a symbol into the fire.

Burning my priestly collar was an expression of death, addressing parts of me that reinforced the postures of perfecting, producing, and performing. It was a declaration that the

Christian world that had shaped me so profoundly would no longer be my center of gravity. It was a declaration that my fifteen-year vocational journey as a pastor was over.

And it was about so much more than just this thread of my story. I was actually destroying every collar in my life. Collars control and constrain. Collars choke and mute and tame. Confronting the taming of women in her book *Untamed,* Glennon Doyle writes, "Glennon, you're a goddam cheetah." As the flames devoured my collar and I watched with my maybe-cheetah-print sarong draped over my shoulders, I chuckled to myself and thought something similar: "Ben, you're a fucking jaguar." I was done being muted. Done being tamed. *There are just too many wilds I'm destined to wander, too many songs I'm meant to sing for me to remain sedated and domesticated.*

As I watched the flames devour the paper collar, I remembered Nayla at the zoo. And the mascot rules. And how you can't keep big cats in the garage. I thought about what Tall Tim had said a few weeks earlier when I told him that I was going to burn the collar. He recalled the superhero Captain Marvel. From a young age, she had a collar around her neck. They told her it gave her protection. They told her it gave her power. But one day she discovered that it actually restricted her power. It interfered with who she truly was. And so she removed it. That's when she found and unleashed her true power.

Ceremonial Grounds

After the warmth of the fire ceremony, I woke to a cold, cloudy day. I was immediately aware of my empty stomach. It had been a full day since my last meal. I slowly packed up all of my things before joining the rest of the group. As the guides led us in a brief farewell ritual, I looked at everyone's faces. People were feeling all sorts of things—anticipation, fear, sadness, exhaustion. We soon went our separate ways, spreading into the many hidden offshoot canyons. I was excited to arrive back at the campsite I had chosen, or that had chosen me, the day before. It would be my home for the next three days.

I set up my tarp over a flat spot. It took a while due to my amateur knot skills. I pulled out my sleeping bag and pad, as well as a few other items, and then I reorganized my pack. I took out my water filter and water containers to fill up. As I approached the nearby stream, I could hear one of Knight's reminders ringing in my ears. *"If nothing is happening here, make yourself even more vulnerable."* So that's exactly what I did: I got naked and immersed myself in the frigid stream—a self-baptism, marking my yearning to be born again.

A little while later, in the clearing where I had first seen the shimmering light, right next to where I set up the tarp, I spontaneously began to move pinecones. Before I knew it, I had cleared an aisle twenty-five yards long, stretching from a narrow, doorlike gap between two trees to a circular area where I laid out the foundations of what became an altar—a thick decaying log; the collection of bones (reassembled according to my best anatomical guesses); variously sized stones I had collected that were shaped like a warrior, buffalo, and lion; and a vibrant bouquet of fresh wildflowers.

The aisle. The altar. The canopy of trees. It was a sanctuary. A temple. And it would be the *spot of time* where, a few days later, I would have one of the most powerful experiences of my life.

Go Fast to Go Slow

Throughout the day I enjoyed the quiet solitude and the space for imaginative play. I was intentionally opening myself to whatever conversation or experience I needed to have. But as the night approached I started to really feel my vulnerability. It was the fasting. I was hungry. I was fatigued. A chill set in my bones. I had dabbled in fasting before, but never like this.

There is a long exploration of fasting in spiritual traditions. Jesus fasted in the wilderness for forty days and forty nights, and following suit, the Desert Fathers and Desert Mothers of early Christianity incorporated fasting into their ascetic practices. My own exposure to fasting was mostly associated with the Christian season of Lent, the forty-day period that leads up to the commemoration of Jesus' death and resurrection on Good Friday and Easter Sunday. While many Catholics fast from meat (land and sky varieties!) on Fridays during Lent—hence the popular Friday fish fry tradition in some communities—other Christians who observe Lent choose their own fasting protocols. Giving up alcohol. Or perhaps coffee, as I once did (regrettably, when we had two young toddlers at home). Some use the religious fasting prompt as an opportunity to try on a new diet that includes avoiding certain foods.

Muslims are even more legendary when it comes to fasting. During Ramadan, billions of Muslims around the world fast from sunup to sundown. A complete fast. No food. No water. (No sex either!). Buddhist traditions, meanwhile, demonstrate a variety of fasting practices, such as vegetarianism, one meal a day, or no food after lunch. Judaism, likewise, has the kosher dietary practices as well as various types of fasting. And some traditions say that if you drop the Torah scrolls, you have to fast for forty days. If others are in the room where it happens, they can volunteer to split the time with you. (Moral of the story: don't drop the scrolls!). Indigenous Amazonian communities, meanwhile, have developed elaborate fasting diets, or *dietas,* that accompany plant medicine ceremonies.

That fasting is beneficial was widely understood long before the calorie-cutting technique of intermittent fasting became trendy. In its more ancient forms, fasting isn't about your figure, it's about drawing closer to the divine. Every moment of hunger or thirst is an opportunity to turn to spirit, to soul, to meaning for sustenance instead of thoughtlessly satiating an impulse by consuming food or drink. Your stomach is not your savior. As Jesus put it, *Humans cannot live by bread alone, but by every word that comes from the mouth of God.*

In many religious and cultural traditions, fasting is also often an expression of mourning. Sorrow swallows the normal urge to eat. A family member is sick or dying. Or a tragedy has hit an entire community. Fasting is also a fitting practice as a symbolic observance of one's own inevitable death. Fasting moves against the grain of so much of our death-avoiding behavior. It connects us with our own frailty and mortality as our bodies weaken in the absence of food.

By teaching us to control physical urges to eat, many traditions believe that fasting opens up new states of consciousness in which perception expands, receptivity to dreams and visions increases, and unity with nature and other beings is experienced. But whether it leads to ecstatic experiences or not, fasting is an opportunity to examine the interior world—questions of identity, purpose, belonging, service. It also grows gratitude.

Over the course of a few days, abstaining from food was difficult, but I could tell it was working on me. In the absence of food and coffee (oh, delicious hot coffee!), I noticed gratitude surging through me. For Cherie and the kids. For my friends. For life. I felt a thinning too. Not of my body (though that was the case), but of the veil between earth and heaven. I felt drawn into the great conversation that takes place in that canyon day after day between the stream and the rock walls, the birds and the trees. I banged the small hand drum I brought. I sang at the top of my lungs. I whispered. I spoke in rhyme. My stomach was empty, but already on my first night alone, I felt like I was being devoured by the depths of the canyon.

The Walking Obituary

The next day I woke up to the buzz of a hummingbird zipping around my tarp. She had been a frequent visitor since I first arrived. I was hungry and cold. I looked at my shoes and socks, soaked from an evening stroll the night before. *Sunshine would be nice,* I thought, before settling into the moment. The stillness of the wild. The bubbling stream and gentle breeze. The dripping pine trees.

Throughout the day, I was in dreamtime. Flowing up the canyon for a short walk (never too far) with a new song on my tongue, then down the temple aisle to the altar, where I tended to the objects I had placed there. Over to the gulch, where a pile of rocks was the checkpoint that Dr. Neil and I had to visit and rearrange each day to let one another know we were okay. Back to my sleeping bag for warmth and rest, talking with trees, fallen and alive, along the way. During one excursion I found a massive hawk feather, which quickly made its way to the altar. When the sun peeked through the clouds, I sat still. I wrote in my journal. I waited. At one point, I heard Dr. Neil in the distance, howling. *He's all in,* I thought to myself, and smiled.

Dusk approached while I was out singing and drumming in the canyon, longing for something magical to happen. It started to rain and I headed back to my tarp. But just before I got there, the temple invited me in. I stood at the entryway and suddenly I knew what I needed to do.

I needed to reflect on each year of my life by performing a sort of walking obituary. To honor and grieve all that had been. And create an opening for what was yet to come.

I pick up the walking stick I adopted earlier. And I begin to walk down the pinecone-lined aisle. As I approach the altar of wild things, I try to recall the first year of my life. No memories come to mind, but I know: *I am a newborn. I've got young parents and a one-year-old brother. I am born into love.* I circle the altar and return to the top of the aisle.

Now coming back down the path, *I am one. A few months later my little brother is born,* I remember as I wind around the collection of wildflowers and rocks on the decaying log. Then a second lap. *I'm two.* I try to fill in other details from old photos.

Again: *I'm three. I run out into the middle of the street. A car slams on the brakes, just missing me. I'm alive. It's a miracle!*

I'm four now. I bring my brand-new Inspector Gadget doll for a show-and-tell, against my mom's advice, and someone pulls one of the go-go-gadget legs out too far. It's broken. I'm crushed.

There in the temple, in the dark woods, in a lonely canyon under the gentle rain, I am walking through the years of my life.

I'm five and we move to the suburbs. My baby brother is born. Elementary school friends, field trips, Sunday school.

Later, in middle school, *I go to camp for a week every summer. I pass notes in class. I'm listening to Boys II Men and Pearl Jam. I have my first kiss with Amanda at the movie theater during* Mrs. Doubtfire.

In the canyon, I laugh. I'm in awe of the gift of life.

Still walking, *There are high school jobs and sports, dances and breakups, and all the advantages I have as a white male that I'm completely unaware of at the time. I deliver pizzas. I dedicate my life to Jesus.*

A few steps later, *I'm eighteen and off to college. I love my college experience.* But in the temple where I'm drenched by the now-heavy rain, I feel something else too: resentment. I'm angry and confused. Those years also feel small and constraining. I missed out on so much of the world. *Why did I go to this conservative Christian college?* I ask myself. Because my parents did. And my grandparents. And I wanted to please them. It was my damn reverent, obedient cadet again!

But then it hits me as I circle the dry bones: Every aspect of my story is an inextricable part of who I am.

College is the place where I develop my taste for the transcendent.

This season sets me on a path to live a life of service.

It's where I meet Nico, my anam cara.

And above all, it is where at the age of eighteen I meet Cherie, the woman who would become my life partner at the young age of twenty-two, the woman I am still with; evolving, changing, and expanding with; growing old with; the woman I love.

At that moment, almost halfway through my life, I'm hit with a piercing gratitude. I lose it. My tears join the rain. I'm weeping at the awareness of her great love for me across the years, and for the gift that it is to love her.

An instant later, I'm laughing because I still have twenty more long years to walk through!

Some laps later, *I move to Seattle. I meet strangers who become lifelong friends. I take risks. I start things. I start a church and create a community center that helps and heals.* As I walk, I wonder why I was always trying to grow up so fast.

One lap, *My daughter Evie is born.* On the next, *My son Jackson arrives. I can't hold back the tears. I play flag football. Lots of beautiful and hard conversations over good coffee and beer.* After a couple laps, *a condom breaks* (too much information?), *and nine months later, in the midst of grieving with heartbroken friends who just lost their newborns, Cherie delivers our daughter Zara into the world. We weep; we celebrate.*

I'm tapping into leadership and creativity I didn't know I had. I'm helping people. I hurt people. I'm hurt. I'm flying. I crash. And I burn out.

I keep walking. *If you don't have your heart, you have nothing* calls me to adventure. *I pick up the pieces through* Grace, Space, Pace. *I leave behind the roles that defined me, but then I relapse to my former ways. I fixate on my career. I want out of my job. But jaguar shows me in a dream there is much more to leave. I'm unlearning so much. It's painful. It's healing. Nico is by my side. Tall Tim too. An owl visits me and I talk to stones. The wind whispers my name and I hug a cactus. I sit at a bar with my dad. Cherie and the kids lay their hands on me and send me away. I'm on a quest. I burn my collar. I'm alone. I baptize myself and build a temple.*

Now I'm here. Beneath the ponderosa pines and the cloud-covered stars. Circling an altar of wood and bone and wildflowers. In this spot of time, in the presence of God or the universe or creator or great spirit or soul—in the presence of The One Who Has Always Been With Me.

I walk through everything. All the joy and sorrow, bitterness and gratitude. All the growing, searching, shedding, and wondering who I am and why I'm here. After thirty-eight laps—thirty-eight years—it is clear to me that all my attempts to perform in particular ways to receive love and to belong are no longer needed. They never were. My search for self-worth in success, my preoccupation with perfection, my efforts to please others, and all the ways I got lost in the lie of *Possession-Control-Mastery*—these ways may have served me in the first half of life, even as they caused me suffering. But these ways will not carry me forward.

In that moment, I'm soaked in rain and tears, my laughter echoing off the canyon walls. No doubt I would look insane to any passerby. But I have become an ancient man, a present man, an eternal man. I am more alive than I have ever been. Because I've contended with my fleeting life. I've faced my many deaths and my inevitable death. My death is complete. And I am reborn.

I feel a deep power within me.

A conviction, a certainty.

That all of life is a gift.

And I've never been alone.

And I belong to everyone and everything.

That I've received so much love.

And I have so much love to give.

After thirty-eighty laps, after thirty-eight years, I know deeply: *My heart once was lost. But now it is found.*

I got my heart back.

PHASE THREE
Rising to Wholeness

On my final morning alone at my campsite, the hummingbird visited me one last time. During each of her previous visits, she had the habit of circling around the outside of my tarp before zipping over to a nearby tree where she would hover over what looked like a knobby cone-shaped growth on a branch just above my head.

This time was different. She was spending more time in the branches. That's when it dawned on me what was going on in the tree. The knobby thing on the branch wasn't part of the tree. It was a nest! As I stood on my tiptoes, I could see a tiny beak grasping upward. A tiny chick just hatched open into new life, new possibility. It felt familiar.

My arrival to the wilderness quest had begun with the two dead chicks on the path and a dead bird outside my room window. My arrival to the campsite was marked by scattered bones. Now, a new arrival was being marked by the presence of this hatchling—my entry into the Rising to wholeness phase of the journey.

This last segment of the quest begins the instant you overcome the final obstacle and accomplish the great task. After you retrieve your heart, you are tasked with the Rising phase's threefold mission of bringing the wholeness you've attained back home, sharing this treasure with others, and cultivating stillness so you never forget what you found. The singular duty behind these three responsibilities is to integrate your discoveries with the world you've always belonged to.

It is an immense challenge, but assistance will once again arrive. Because you will not be the only one who has become aligned with your heart. Already events and opportunities and characters beyond your awareness will have been conspiring to ensure that you fulfill your destiny upon your return home.

The birth of the hummingbird—occurring just after my death in the temple as I walked through the years of my life—was propelling me into this next, final leg of the journey. As I packed my things up to return to the group in eager anticipation of breaking my fast, I received one more parting gift. I lifted the ground tarp to fold it and noticed out of the corner of my eye something softly floating back to the ground. It was a tiny, fluffy, yellow and green hummingbird feather. I picked it up, looked back up at the nest, and had one last thought before I hiked out:

I'm born again.

Now, I just needed to learn how to fly.

"We may become strangers to those who thought they knew us, but at least we are no longer strangers to ourselves."

—James Hollis, *The Middle Passage*

"He has yet to confront society with his ego-shattering, life-redeeming elixir, and take the return blow of reasonable queries, hard resentment, and good people at a loss to comprehend."

—Joseph Campbell,
The Hero with a Thousand Faces

7

RETURN HOME

"It's gone. It's done," says Frodo. He's referring to the ring, and the grueling quest he embarked on to destroy it, in this scene near the end of *Return of the King*. Mission accomplished, thanks to the creature Gollum, who just delivered the ring into the belly of Mount Doom.

"Yes, Mister Frodo, it's over now," replies Sam, his faithful friend.

The two unlikely heroes share a brief moment of relief, until a volcanic explosion jolts them from behind, reminding them of their predicament. They are stranded on a rock on the side of a rapidly deteriorating mountain. They realize they aren't going to make it out alive—that it is, as Frodo says, "the end of all things" for them. So they do the one thing they would do if they could somehow escape that fiery slope. They return home.

In their imaginations, they visit the Shire, the Brandywine River, and Bag End. They see Gandalf's fire, the lights, the Party Tree, and Rosie Cotton dancing, with ribbons in her hair. With home in their hearts and tears in their eyes, these two soul friends embrace. They won't really get to return home—or will they?

Suddenly, in the distance, a convocation of giant eagles appears, soaring through the sky. They airlift Frodo and Sam out of the rising sea of lava, setting them on the path home. Before long, the Hobbits will be sipping on some pints back at the Green Dragon.

The Magic Flight

This scene from the final installment of the *Lord of the Rings* movie trilogy captures a consistent mythical feature. The *Magic Flight*. It starts the moment *after* the hero has attained the sought-after treasure. Having discovered a powerful hidden place or magical object—the key to immortality, an elixir for eternal life, the fountain of youth—the hero must now escape from the protective powers that guard what they have just discovered or conquered.

Frodo and Sam leave behind the lava of Mount Doom.

Luke Skywalker escapes the exploding Death Star.

In a way, the entire *Odyssey* is a magical flight home for Odysseus after victory at Troy.

The *Magic Flight* is the first part of the return home—the initial step of the Rising phase. Just as the mythical heroes must outlast or outwit the pursuing forces, when you get your heart back you must face opposition that attempts to prevent you from delivering back to society what you've discovered. Once upon a time, you experienced resistance to *leaving* home, and now comes the resistance to *returning* home. The first form of resistance to returning is usually . . . *yourself.*

The Refusal of Return

At one point, before your descent into the subterranean space of darkness, wilderness, and death in search of your soul, you crossed a threshold. You left the dilapidated house. You *Let Go.* And now, after recovering your heart, you must cross back over the return threshold to come back to everyday life, to the ordinary world, with your newfound wholeness.

This is no simple task. David Whyte captures this dynamic in his poem, "Revelation Must Be Terrible." Returning home is difficult because you are now wide awake. You've seen your true face, and you can no longer hide it. You've heard your true voice, and you can never silence it again. You will need to figure out what bringing your heart back will look like, but first you face the more general challenge of reintegration with the community and the world you left behind. Confronted with this next difficult requirement, it is tempting to refuse to return. You wonder: *Maybe it's just easier to stay in these murky depths and dark wonders of soul initiation. Maybe I should just keep all this preciousness to myself.*

We witness this resistance to returning across the ancient stories. After Peter, a disciple of Jesus, briefly witnessed his teacher's radiant transformation on a mountainside, he wanted to set up a camp where he could enjoy the moment forever. No need to return to the trials and tribulations of the real world!

Similarly, the Zohar, Kabbalist Judaism's main text, features a creation story that captures the soul's hesitation to get tainted by the world. A Soul responds to the Creator's assignment: "Lord of the world, I am content to remain in this realm, and have no wish to depart to some other, where I shall be in thralldom, and become stained."

Meanwhile, the Hindu warrior-king Muchukunda experiences a literal and figurative awakening from a something-million-year nap, looks at the mess of humanity, and decides to find a cave higher in the mountains. Rather than returning, he decides to retreat even farther from the world. Honestly, who can blame him?

I felt this same pull. The pull to remain in the exotic underworld of wandering and dreams. I didn't want this sprawling season of feasting on mystical moments to end. I had endured so much to get my heart back. Now that I had it, I wanted to protect it, to keep it safe.

That's how I felt the morning after my walking obituary on the last day of my solo. *Do I have to go back to the busy world beyond the canyon rim? It would be easier to stay here, far away from the challenges and demands of relationships, the practical questions about where to work and where to live. I have everything I need here (except for maybe chips and salsa), especially when the sun finally peeks through the clouds to warm my face and dry my socks.*

Maybe I could grow old in this canyon. I could learn to hunt. I could figure out other survival skills. After all, I've seen the movie Castaway—*if Tom Hanks could do it, I could do it too!*

Our guides Knight and Bear warned us about this spiritual gravity that would draw us to remain in the dreamtime of the canyon before we set out on our solo experiences. In anticipation of this seduction, they told us to leave behind an object at base camp. Something that represented our lives beyond the canyon rim. An item that, when we remembered it, would energetically pull us out of the solo, out of the canyon, back to our people. My tethering object was a mug. I used it for tea, oatmeal, and soup during the quest. But back home it was also my go-to coffee mug, which is why I left it behind at base camp.

During my last day alone, when I was weighing my options, I thought about the mug. Like Frodo and Sam, I could imagine myself back home. The warm, coffee-filled mug is in my hand. The morning sunlight streams through the windows, filtered by the Japanese maple tree outside. Cherie is across from me, the kids are sifting through a Lego pile on the floor between us, variously listening and chatting as Cherie and I talk about what we have to do that day and how we are doing, about the light and heavy questions we are carrying.

I thought about this everyday scene. It was so ordinary, but it was also so vibrant and alive. I wanted to go home. I was ready. Even as a part of me wanted to stay in the stage of solitude and introspection, in the mystery and questions, I also knew that I could only really know and claim what I had discovered at the bottom of that canyon—at the bottom of myself—by returning home.

For a long time, I had been waiting for something to be born. It was.

I *was.*

And now it was time to figure out how to bring this new sense of aliveness and awake-ness, this being-put-back-together wholeness and love into the world.

But first I needed to escape the canyon alive.

Destroying the Temple of My Former Life

My *Magic Flight* out of the canyon began before dawn on the final morning of my solo, a few hours before I met the newly hatched hummingbird.

I woke up nearly one hundred hours into fasting and couldn't fall back asleep. There was something I needed to do. I got out of my sleeping bag, added some layers, grabbed my headlamp, and walked over to the temple. It had been my ceremonial space for the past three days, the place I had faced death by walking through all the years of my life two nights earlier. I began to dismantle the temple. I destroyed the altar first. The rotting logs went back to the gulch, the stones to a rocky washout. I returned the flowers, mushrooms, and pine needles to the forest floor. I re-scattered the bones. Then, by kicking around the pinecones, I erased the long aisle that I had walked up and down thirty-eight times.

On one level, it was a standard backpacking "Leave No Trace" practice. But it was also more than that. It was a way of breaking any power that sacred place might claim over me. That place was—I realized as I tore it down—the *Temple of My Former Life*. What happened there, in the rain, and everything from the years I walked through, would always be with me and in me. But I needed to begin the process of Rising, that is, of transforming the gratitude, the grief, the glory of the past—including all of the wild, mystical moments—into an offering of love in the present. Destroying the temple was an acknowledgement that my center of gravity is not located anywhere in my history. My North Star is not something I *once* did, not some previous accomplishment or failure, not anything that happened to me in my past. It is here and now.

The Ascent Home

I finished destroying the temple as the sun was rising and crawled back into my sleeping bag to rest for another hour or two. Soon the hummingbird mother and child greeted me. I packed up my camp and then reunited with Dr. Neil at our designated spot. He was glowing, and said I was too. Despite empty stomachs and full backpacks, we started bounding back to base camp, our retrieved hearts overflowing with love, our eyes alive with new vision.

But, almost immediately, it was as if some force was thwarting our return. Low clouds descended into the canyon, inhibiting visibility. It was pouring rain and the streams we previously hopped over casually had become fast-moving rivers. We made a wrong turn and headed in the opposite direction for fifteen minutes before we realized it. We were lost, soaked, and starving. We had to hack our way through thick brush in order to avoid dangerous river crossings. And yet we were laughing, content, grateful.

Eventually we made it back to camp. We were the last ones. The welcome was warm—comforting hugs, hot tea, and an introductory meal of avocado with lemon and cayenne, jicama, and a light soup to ease our emergence from hunger.

Over the next few days, we shared our stories of what we had left behind or who we had become. For some, the quest was an initiation into the unknown. For others, it marked an arrival to wholeness. Meanwhile, the threats to our escape from the canyon continued, each environmental obstacle a symbol of the challenges of returning home and reintegrating into community.

On the day of our reunion, the rain wouldn't let up and the river water levels rose. We wondered about the deteriorating back roads that had delivered us to the trailhead at the canyon rim. *Would they even be passable?* We were all soaked. We set up tarps for cover. Our guides got a fire going. Some of us hunted for dry wood while others peeled the bark off wet logs to dry by the fire.

The next morning we woke up to a thick blanket of snow. The once-dry washouts around our base camp were flooded with frigid water. Our guides, who had led dozens of wilderness quests, had never experienced anything like it. "What is the canyon still trying to teach us?" our guide Bear asked. Many of the questers, however, were done with the canyon's lessons and growing increasingly anxious about whether or not we would be able to leave on time. But the weather was out of our control, the guides reminded us. We warmed our feet, socks, and gloves by the fire. We shared more wonder-filled quest stories. And, finally, late in the afternoon, the rain stopped, the sun began to shine through, and birds began to sing again. That night was the coldest yet, but the night sky finally became clear. A million brilliant stars were visible, a hopeful sign for our morning departure. The next day, the sun was out, the sky was blue, and the streams had subsided. *We can leave!* Everyone was relieved, and I could not wait to see my family.

We fueled up with breakfast, packed one last time, and erased the evidence of our base camp. Our ascent out of the enchanted canyon began. I felt so energized. Like a gazelle I swiftly climbed up the trail. But the challenges weren't over. We had to help exhausted members of our group, jump a car with a dead battery, repair sections of storm-washed roads, and even do some off-roading to bypass huge pits that had formed. *The Magic Flight* continued!

Once we made it back to the main road where the rest of the cars were parked, we held a brief closing ceremony. Just like that, our time was over. As I got a ride to the tiny airport where I would board a small eight-seat plane, I turned on my phone for the first time in almost two weeks, and I was catapulted back into the world. Hundreds of text messages, calls, and photos of the familiar world I had left behind. I FaceTimed Cherie and got to see the kids run off the school bus. I cried. It was so good to see their beautiful faces.

A little while later, during my layover in Denver, I sat at a bar and ate a bacon cheeseburger that I washed down with the biggest beer they would serve me while watching *Game of Thrones* on my iPhone. I couldn't help but laugh at the ridiculousness of it all. The scene was so far from where I had begun my day. I had ascended a remote trail to a muddy road to a rural gravel road to a pothole-filled highway to one airport and another and, finally, to this bustling, bright, fast food–filled place. I wondered what the canyon was doing at that exact moment. *The humming-birds humming. The stream . . . streaming. The rocks . . . rocking. Everything being exactly what it is, and nothing else.*

After another flight and an Uber ride, it was nearly midnight when I arrived home. Flower petals and candles lit my path to the front door. The door opened. Cherie was there. Before we touched, she welcomed me across the threshold by surrounding me with the smoke of sage, just like Vanya had done after the death lodge. We held each other. I showered for the first time in almost two weeks. We traded stories, and then we were in each other's arms again.

The next morning, I was greeted by the sweet faces and excited voices of my children. We sat in the living room, light streaming in, and I sipped my first cup of coffee. From the mug that I had carried into the canyon.

I was home.

Home Is Where the Heart Is

My friend recently told me about her friend who had open-heart surgery. He had made a full recovery and was already back at the things he loved the most, one of which was running long-distance races. But, she said, he was also up to some new things. She didn't get into details, but said he had new interests, new cravings. He told her that his doctors had said this is a common result of open-heart surgery—it is a total reset that leads the surgery recipient into entirely new ways of being in the world.

It makes sense that a person changes after such a dramatic operation. Because the heart stops beating for a moment during surgery. Just like when we die. And then it starts again. The operation is a kind of rebirth.

Getting your heart back again leads to the same kind of reset and rebirth. You no longer move through the world in the same way you used to. You return to the same home, but you are a different person. Things feel a bit off. They don't quite fit anymore. That's because you've discovered your true home:

it's your heart. And so the challenge becomes figuring out how your heart-home fits back in your old neighborhood, with all of its noise and nosiness, complacency and conflicts. It doesn't take long for the discrepancy between your retrieved, reset heart and the home you left behind to become apparent.

There was a kindness to the initial days of my return. The touch of my beloved and snuggles with my kids. Reunions with friends who were curious about my quest. And lots of hot things to enjoy—coffee, showers, food.

But the return was also abrasive. Like Rip Van Winkle waking from his twenty-year slumber in the Catskills, I was bewildered by the strange world I had reentered. The screaming presence of screens everywhere, the bombardment of texts and emails. The pace of the day. Errands to run. Little conflicts between the kids. The needs and demands of others. The world above the canyon was closing in on me.

Feeling overwhelmed by the ordinary is a common experience. According to Campbell, "The first problem of the returning hero is to accept as real, after an experience of the soul-satisfying vision of fulfillment, the passing joys and sorrows, banalities and noisy obscenities of life. Why re-enter such a world?"

I had my moments of asking that question, especially as the canyon started to feel like a distant dream. I missed its silence, solitude, and stillness. But missing the canyon was representative of a much deeper ache. After all, I wasn't just returning home after two weeks in the wild, but from a Leaving and Falling process that had begun nearly five years earlier on that rainy morning run. The wilderness quest was just the capstone. But my homecoming had been years in the making.

With each new day back home, I became more aware of how massive the challenge of returning would be. And it didn't take me long to feel the weight of the main question that meets anyone who has reclaimed their heart at this moment:

Now what?

This single question carried with it a thousand other questions:

What does this all mean for me?

How do I translate this soulful experience into daily life?

How do I live in a heart-forward way as it relates to family, vocation, relationships, money, choices, starting things, stopping things, etc.?

How do I channel the overwhelming love and gratitude I discovered into this waking world amid the demands of parenting, the daily responsibilities of home and work, the rhythms of relationships and friendship?

In all the questions, my core conviction was that *you can take the man out of the canyon, but you can't take the canyon out of the man.* The canyon quest—and the canyon years—had left an indelible mark on me. This experience defined my new reality. It was a new foundation for everything.

William Stafford calls this the "thread" in his poem "The Way It Is," which the quest guides had read to us during our final days as a sort of blessing or prayer. There is an unchanging thread that weaves its way through all the things that change on the surface of our lives. While it is invisible to others, you pursue it, even as things come and go, begin and end, fail and succeed. As long as you hold on to it, you won't get lost. The great challenge of returning home is to figure out how you will hold on to the thread.

X & Y

During our final hours in the canyon, as we huddled around the fire trying to stay warm, our guides prepared us for how we could follow the thread discovered in the soul realm as we transitioned back into the ordinary world. They presented searching questions for us to hold at the conclusion of our wilderness quest—questions that are also fitting for consideration after a day Wander or at the close of a soulful season of life:

> *Who went on the quest?*
> *What happened out there?*
> *Who returns?*
> *What healing gift do you bring back to your people?*
> *What remains in the mystery?*

Then, after posing these questions, they started doing algebra . . . Or, at least, that's what it seemed like when they first started talking about the letters X and Y.

"X is what got you here. X is who you were. It is ego," explained Knight. "Y is what happened in the canyon. What came alive, what you discovered here. Y is soul."

Bear jumped in. "Your X life is waiting for you above the canyon rim. But how will you not leave Y down here? So much will work against you to erase what happened. To forget it. To quiet it. How will you keep Y alive?"

The point isn't to eliminate X, your ego. That's actually impossible. But after undergoing this transformational experience, it's time for X to be in service to Y, for ego to follow the wisdom of soul. Ego is no longer in charge—it makes a lousy master—but instead it is time for ego to support soul in expressing its calling in the world.

Both guides explained how we would need to be intentional in order to keep Y alive alongside X. We needed a program to help us move through the world, to keep Y alive, to carry the thread forward.

The program looks different for each person. As my daughter taught me when she began to fall in love with house plants, each particular plant needs a different program—water amount and frequency, location and light exposure, soil quantity and consistency. The same principle applies to how we keep Y alive in an X-oriented world.

While it is indeed different strokes for different folks, there are some main categories that are part of any program to keep Y alive. Ritual Practices, relationships, decisions, and projects (which we'll cover in the next chapter).

Ritual Practices

From the day we arrived in the canyon until the day we departed, our guides cautioned us against stepping on the crypto. I was confused. *How exactly does one step on a digital currency?* But then I figured out that they were referring to cryptobiotic soil, a slow-growing desert surface layer consisting of living organisms and inorganic soil matter that is crucial to desert life. Desert crypto, which has a sponge-like look and texture, resists erosion by wind and water, and does all sorts of other stuff to encourage diverse plant growth in the desert. It's also extremely fragile, which is why our guides constantly reminded us to be on the lookout and not harm this foundational desert element.

Crypto makes the desert grow green.

Ritual Practices are the crypto for the task of returning home and the Rising phase of the quest. They keep you connected to where you have been, what you have discovered, and who you are becoming—just as they have throughout the entire quest. To give up on practices at this point is to trample all over the desert crypto that has empowered your growth.

As the pressures and pace of the world come roaring back at you, being intentional about carving out time for grounding practices is critical. It can be solitude, fasting, dreamwork, yoga, or something else. Something you've carried with you. Or something new. It can be a ceremonial or ritual space like a Wander with a beginning, middle, end. It can be revisiting your death lodge. Whatever it is, these Ritual Practices are a space to speak back to the mystery, to continue to receive what was discovered, and to pledge your allegiance to Y, your soul.

In the months following the canyon, I continued with many of my practices. I tended to new dreams, like the owl dreams that kept coming at me. I regularly visited my *spot of time* in the woods. And I explored other wild places, alone and with my family. I also felt the power of music in new ways and enjoyed listening, singing, and spontaneously dancing.

But the biggest game changer was meditation. Immediately after I returned I began to practice a new technique for twenty minutes twice a day. It was a gentle and spacious way to carry forward all of the wildness that had grown within me. Questions that had haunted me previously—about jobs, moving, money—were still there, but meditation helped me carry them differently. If my mind started to spiral in fear and stress, meditation would bring me back to my breath and to the present moment. And by being in the present moment it was as if I was simultaneously back beneath the ponderosa pines, completely absorbed in the knowledge that love is who I am and why I'm here.

Ritual Practices grounded me in love. They also rooted me in contentment instead of worry, as I reflected in my journal:

> But I notice worry's growing silence when I appoint my soul
> as guide. The air clears and the birdsong emerges. My efforts
> to force the path straight into the clearing relax as I welcome
> the disorientation of the thickets, tall grasses, and towering
> groves. In these lost spaces I find my way. And worry is
> welcome, but it must follow and yield to the directionless
> direction of my soul.

I didn't have answers to the questions about the arrangement of things on the surface of my life. These questions had troubled me for a long time when X ran the show, but they no longer held their distracting, anxiety-provoking power. It was as if they had been sloughed off by my time in the canyon. I was no longer getting tossed about by these questions because I was anchored in my heart where I had everything I needed and, as a result, experienced orientation in the disorientation. Certainty in the uncertainty. Knowing in the unknown.

Relationships

In addition to necessitating Ritual Practices, the process of reintegration also has significant implications for relationships.

On a very basic level, one of the first relational questions you have upon returning home is, as one of my fellow canyon questers asked our guides, *Who can I tell these stories to?* In response, the guides cautioned us about what we choose to share and with whom we choose to share it. Yes, some of us have the *anam cara* support of people like Cherie, Nico, or Tall Tim, who have become our trusted companions along the way. But it is likely that many people in our circles have not gone on this interior journey and won't understand.

These soulful experiences—all that we discover—are a treasure, not to be easily dispersed among people who don't get it. Campbell asks, "Why attempt to make plausible or even interesting, to men and women consumed with passion, the experience of transcendental bliss?" Jesus puts it a bit more starkly: "Do not cast your pearls before swine." (*Whoa, Jesus, that's harsh*). If you do choose to share with others, a more formal, ceremonial setting might be in order, perhaps even one that invites similar vulnerability from others. Ultimately, it is more important to embody your discoveries than to talk about them. *Don't tell what happened. Show it.* Besides, even if you wanted to, you could not fully translate the mysteries of soul.

Beyond the question of who to share your stories with, there is a deeper, more difficult reality that anyone returning home after a long, inward adventure must be aware of: the true version of you that comes back may no longer be compatible with the world that you left behind. It's like the feeling of returning home from college for the first time, times a thousand, where you see old high school friends and have a sense that this life doesn't fit anymore. *Your heart, remember, has been retrieved, reset, reborn.*

On the more extreme end of the changes you've undergone is the possibility that your awakening may lead to the end of some relationships. You've been changing this whole time, shedding unhealthy layers, but upon your return home, there is a sharpened clarity about it. It's finally apparent that your marriage is over. It's time for separation from your family of origin. You must end certain friendships that have become lifeless or toxic. (Important Note: This does not mean abandoning your sacred duty to your children!).

Some of these necessary relational shifts will be immediately obvious. Others will take some time to surface as you more fully express who you've become. You will make decisions people do not understand. Your actions may look reckless or impulsive to others. Only you know their true source. People will have all sorts of strong feelings stirred up when you choose to no longer perform the Impostor role that they are used to. *A prophet is not welcome in his hometown,* Jesus said.

The process of navigating relationships is hard, but as our guides reminded us, *If you're not disturbing people, you're not doing your work right now.* Your challenge is to discern which disturbed people to move toward because they just need time to adjust, and which people to move away from because they will forever refuse to let you be anyone other than who you've always been to them. Establishing new, healthy boundaries in relationships and observing how people respond to them will aid in your discernment process.

One word of caution about the unavoidable changes in the landscape of your relationships. While the difficult but necessary ending of relationships will be called for, you must also be aware of the temptation to withdraw from those who are your people, people who have been supportive of you even if they haven't fully understood your journey, people to whom you still belong and are called. So don't just ditch people. In other words, look out for a kind of spiritual arrogance that can flare up here—*I've changed, no one else has!* This is a dangerous path to go down.

Your people might not speak your new language, but they love you, always have. Even when you have been unable to see yourself, they have been able to see parts of who you truly are. They keep you grounded. They keep your ego in check and draw you beyond just talk and into embodiment, beyond preaching to practice. They don't let you bypass reality and retreat into soul. They bring you out of the cave high in the remote mountains and down into the here and now. You would be wise to not forsake this gift!

Finally, while a return home means the end to some relationships, it also invites the birth of new ones. Returning can be lonely, but you will only get frustrated if you expect your community to understand all that you've been through. If you somehow didn't find *anam cara* companionship yet in your journey (this is rare), you are certainly going to need it now! You're going to need more people, more connections, more spaces. You become a bit of a dual citizen—no single person or social group will be able to hold your desires and dreams. It is critical to expand our relational webs in order to be supported and spurred on in our wholeness.

Decisions, Decisions

Just as navigating relationship shifts and sustaining Ritual Practices are crucial to bringing your heart back home, it is also important to take decisive action.

When you re-emerge from the canyonlands of the Falling phase, you may return with a conviction about some action you need to take—something either you have been toying with for a while or related to a circumstance you haven't even considered changing. A relationship, job, move, hobby, conversation, confrontation, donation. It can be in any area of life.

If you know what you need to do, then you must say yes or say no *immediately,* or mobilize toward that action without delay. Taking decisive action isn't about an ongoing commitment or process. It is about starting or stopping, adding or subtracting. If you refuse to take this one-step action, it can interfere with your way forward.

While I still wanted to quit my job, it wasn't yet possible financially. More importantly, my heart was not yet telling me it was time to leave. But there were a few projects (which we'll cover in the next chapter) I knew I needed to say yes to, and there was one thing I knew it was time to end: my spiritual direction with Tall Tim.

To be clear, ending spiritual direction or therapy or some other form of support is not a prescription for everyone. For some, the return home may require beginning or increasing this kind of accompaniment. I knew, however, that for me it was time for a conclusion with Tall Tim. When I told him about my decision at our second-to-last session, along with stories from my wilderness quest, he understood.

We had been meeting for two years. He had been my underworld companion and guide. But that season had come to an end. He had set me up to walk in the direction I needed going forward, but I sensed I needed a different type of support for this next season. It felt important to take this decisive action in order to clearly distinguish between my Falling into the unknown and Rising to wholeness phases.

One of my quest guides had told me how Carl Jung at one point in his life realized that he was living without a myth, and when he did, he decided to give himself fully to finding it. According to my guide, Jung said that the most important question anyone can ask is: *What myth am I living?* Tall Tim had helped me ask and answer this question. He welcomed all of my confusion and yearning. He affirmed that all the mystical moments and timely omens mattered. He confirmed that my quest was *real*.

For our final spiritual direction session, Tall Tim and I agreed to meet at a small lake near my house that we had walked around numerous times. As I arrived, snippets of conversations we'd had there echoed in my mind. I recalled my frustration, angst, and despair. And I remembered the wonder, gratitude, and juicy questions too. I was grateful for all of it. It had all led me to where I was meant to be—at home in myself, home to love.

Tall Tim was waiting for me on a park bench. He stood up,

towering above me, and we hugged. "Welcome, Cat Man," he said, as he raised one finger like a claw. We laughed. This time we didn't walk. We sat, gazing out at the smooth, shimmering water. Tall Tim reflected back to me all of the struggling and shedding and growing and healing and transforming he had witnessed. I thanked him for his steady support, strong and soft, through a spiritually grueling chunk of my life. What a good kindness!

I'm not sure what else I said, but I do know that when we parted ways, a pair of hawks—one adult, one juvenile—were circling around a tiny, tree-covered island in the distance. And it felt like an image for all that Tall Tim had done for me as a spiritual director. He helped me hatch. He showed me where to find sustenance. He taught me how to unfurl my wings and fly.

Later I scribbled in my journal some of the simple yet profound truths that I had accumulated and carried with me, supported by Tall Tim and others, when I finally arrived back home after five long years away:

Bring joy, be curious, trust the mystery, have patience, persevere, pursue what you want, don't wear masks, be yourself and nobody else, breathe deeply, let comparison inspire, celebrate others, look for teammates, be vulnerable, share your story, don't worry about repeating yourself or always being original. Just be you.

"Don't ask yourself what the world needs. Ask yourself what makes you come alive, and go do that, because what the world needs is people who have come alive."

—Howard Thurman

"The hero shall now begin the labor of bringing the runes of wisdom, the Golden Fleece, or his sleeping princess back into the kingdom of humanity, where the boon may redound to the renewing of the community, the nation, the planet, or the ten thousand worlds."

—Joseph Campbell,
The Hero with a Thousand Faces

8

GIVE YOUR GIFT

The True Treasure

As the Mythical Pattern goes, the hero leaves the ordinary world and descends into the realm of soul where magical powers are encountered and threatening forces are confronted. The hero emerges victorious before coming back home in the closing segment of the journey. But that's not all that happens. There is another aspect that is central to the hero's arrival: returning with a special power. He or she comes back home with a boon—a gift to give.

Myths often speak of this gift as a treasure. And this treasure is often one of the main reasons the adventure begins in the first place. In the Greek myth, Jason embarks on a voyage with a ship full of heroes and retrieves the Golden Fleece. Odin returns with the Mead of the Poets. Sir Percival of the Knights of the Round Table achieves the Holy Grail in the medieval British King Arthur fables (Indiana Jones does too).

In *The Hobbit*, it is the Arkenstone that Bilbo Baggins

discovers in the dragon Smaug's hoard of treasure deep inside the Lonely Mountain.

Meanwhile, the Avengers travel through the multiverse to collect all six of the Infinity Stones to bring half of the planet back to life.

No matter how rare or sparkly or golden the treasure is in these stories, its acquisition is representative of things being made right, of harmony being restored, of getting your heart back. In other words, it's not literally about riches and material things.

The true treasure has always been your heart. Nothing more, nothing less.

This truth bears repeating, even at this late stage in the journey. Especially because there are plenty of misleading guides and distracting messages in the realm of "self-help" and "self-improvement" that confuse the symbolic and literal nature of the hero's treasure. In some of these instances, the true treasure of wholeness and healing is replaced entirely by that of actual, physical treasure like wealth and success.

But it's usually more subtle than that. It often comes in the form of an add-on:

Health *and* wealth.

Get your heart back *and* attain success in your business.

Pursue your passion *and* make tons of money.

Along the way, these achievement-oriented endeavors might include some similar elements to the quest to reclaim your heart, such as letting go of limiting beliefs, being willing to take risks, and making sacrifices—all of which are beneficial approaches to life. But ultimately, any sense of entitlement to actual, material treasure distorts, disrupts, and delays one's arrival at the true destination.

Any time *and* is added, you can veer off course from the pursuit of your heart and into the seduction of *Possession-Control-Mastery.*

Or, as Jesus put it, *No one can serve two masters.*

Rather than helping your truest and deepest self, these supposedly heroic quests for material riches actually hinder your evolution. It's not self-improvement; it's self-diminishment. Because you're still clinging to some external standard, still refusing to surrender.

So, to be clear, the treasure is a symbol . . . Retrieving your heart may come with other kinds of treasure, but this is not the emphasis or expectation. But that's okay. Because the symbolic treasure you find is far more valuable, far more needed. Your treasure is an elixir—medicine for your community and the world. So it's not just something you get. It's something you give. Even more, it's not just something. It is someone. The treasure is *you.*

This brings up two of the main questions that surface in this step of the Rising phase:

What, specifically, is the medicine you are to the world? And how do you deliver it?

Or you could ask, *What is your gift? How do you give it?*

The Sound of the Genuine

To ask these questions is to consider the question of vocation. The word vocation comes from the Latin word *vocare,* meaning "to call." Your vocation is your calling. Your unique contribution to the world. *Who you are and why you are here.*

I had been asking vocational questions for as long as I could remember, and especially during the five years of my quest. However, in my Leaving and Falling, vocational matters became muddled. I lost the clarity I once thought I had. Things I had once poured myself into and thought were at the center of my identity no longer carried the same weight. It was a kind of vocational amnesia in which I could no longer detect any through lines that connected my ways of being, my passions, and my work. I wondered if I would ever have a sense of purpose and focus again.

But when I returned from the wilderness quest, it was as if I had also ascended out of a five-year-long canyon of my life. I could see the horizon before, behind, and all around me. I regained my vocational bearings.

This is a common aspect of finding your way home. Even if you haven't been asking vocational questions already, you are automatically thrust into concerns related to your calling. This is because of the fundamental shift that occurs: you move from being externally referenced to internally referenced. The relative desires, expectations, and suggestions of particular people and society no longer govern what "the good life" looks like. The *Possession-Control-Mastery* program doesn't dictate what you should pursue in the world.

Instead, there is a new baseline for your existence. You've encountered God or the absolute or the universal field or source or soul. You've reconnected with your heart, heard your true voice, and seen your true face—the core, essential you. However you might describe it, this realm is your new reference point. This is the source of your new knowing. This is what guides your actions in the world. You become rooted in soul. Your allegiance is to soul instead of society.

Theologian, mystic, and civil rights leader Howard Thurman called this *the sound of the genuine*. In a 1980 commencement speech at Spelman College, he declared:

> "The sound of the genuine is flowing through you. Don't be deceived and thrown off by all the noises that are a part even of your dreams, your ambitions, so that you don't hear the sound of the genuine in you, because that is the only true guide that you will ever have, and if you don't have that you don't have a thing."

If you don't have your true guide . . . *you don't have a thing.* Or, you could say, *If you don't have your heart, you have nothing.* Getting your heart back hones your ability to detect the sound of the genuine cutting through the noise of society.

Let Your Life Speak

We often must travel through foreign territory before we arrive at a sense of our calling, educator and activist Parker Palmer writes in *Let Your Life Speak*. These strange lands include the terrain we travel through in our seasons of Leaving and Falling. They seem endless. It doesn't feel like we're making much vocational progress. But, in reality, during this disorienting time we develop at least three critical skills that keep us attuned to the sound of the genuine.

First, we learn to slow down. Ever seen someone sprinting down the beach while using a metal detector? I didn't think so. "Slow and low," they say, is the way to go when searching for buried treasure. The same goes for detecting our calling. We can't speed through life or bounce around between things if we want to gain insight about the contribution we are called to make in the world. Nor can we hover far above commitments or explore our options endlessly. We've got to get close to life and take things seriously. This is how we glean from our experiences and learn what to integrate and what to disregard going forward.

Just as it was for me with practicing *Grace, Space, Pace*, getting quiet, and so much more, the slowness of Ritual Practices cultivates within us a Mystical Presence—a powerful combination and foundation for vocation. This intentional work of courting your soul is where your true service begins.

Your calling doesn't come out of nowhere. It always has some continuity with previous aspects of your life. The acorn of a future oak tree has always been within you. The entire quest is an exercise in slowing down and learning to listen to your life. When you let your life speak you start to remember long forgotten interests and recall young dreams you had for your life. What you once considered to be scattered experiences, you now see as a trail of breadcrumbs guiding you to your calling. It turns out that you've always been a healer or storyteller, builder or nurturer, weaver or disrupter, or whatever it is—you've just expressed it in different contexts at different levels with different actions.

As I slowed down, I could detect aspects of my vocation

stretching across my life. My position in my family of origin as the second of four sons called forth my *in-between-ness*. And from that location, my natural *seer* abilities were nurtured. I learned to read a group and sense the needs of individuals in that group. I built bridges. I translated. I adapted. And all these ways of being were expressed again and again beyond my family as I grew into adulthood in how I listened and communicated, how I helped people and fostered community.

I also noticed that there was always a certain kind of *jaguarness* that I brought to all my endeavors. I was consistently working to create and sustain vibrant ecosystems where everyone could thrive and contribute. Just like the jaguar, a keystone species that brings balance. The jaguar controls the food chain by ensuring that rodents don't overpopulate the rainforest and strip it of the seeds and bugs that are the source of tree and plant regeneration. Admittedly, my approach to creating a healthy environment didn't involve ferociously devouring anything or anyone, but I was consistently working to create healthy environments, and I did so with the kind of patience and perseverance that are also characteristic of the jaguar.

The second vocational discernment skill we learn as we wander through these alien lands is that *wounds are wayfinders*. They help us navigate our way toward the treasure we have to offer the world.

I felt pretty dialed in to my vocation before my *If you don't have your heart, you have nothing* burnout moment. I just needed to learn how to express my calling in a more sustainable way. But it was never going to be sustainable as long as I kept running from my wounds. I needed to get acquainted with them, examine them, and tend to them. Not only would this wound work help me go forward, it would allow me to access my essential powers in their fullest form.

It is tempting to only look back at the shining moments of our lives, at the times when any attentive observer would easily confirm that we were exercising our powers, rather than also examining our more difficult experiences. But this ignores the wisdom of our wounds. The painful parts of our pasts—the harm we experienced in our families of origin, the ways we were rejected by our peers, the impairments and illnesses we experienced, the personas we created to get by—are often clues to the contributions that are ours to make.

Just as the entire quest is an exercise in slowing down, it is also a forum for working with our wounds. The darkness illuminates our wounds. The wilderness is a soothing balm. And all the forms of *anam cara* bear witness to our healing.

I spent most of my life avoiding my wounds. I wouldn't even let myself acknowledge that I carried any pain. There were multiple reasons for this. For one, there was a staunch Dutch work ethic and immigrant mentality that insisted your only option is to push through when things are difficult. When something hurts, you need to get over it and keep going. Another reason for ignoring my wounds had to do with a particular way I was wired. As a *seer* I was always so aware of the suffering of others—from oppressive racism and inequity, to devastating disease and death, to fractured families and abusive relationships—and my experience didn't even come close to those realities. So I minimized and ignored the harm I had experienced. But wounds are wounds. All wounds are worth tending to. Or else we end up passing on our pain to our communities, our children, our world.

When I began to welcome my wounds, I not only interrupted the transmission of my pain, but I also gained powerful insight into my vocation. I realized that I remembered those who are ignored and rejected because I felt forgotten, that I could see the unique gifts and contributions of others because I so often felt unseen, and that I fostered belonging and created community because I felt alone and disconnected. This process of wound work refined and strengthened my understanding of my vocational powers. My future contributions would likely resemble my past ones, but they would be more grounded and more whole—not distorted by my own anxious impulses, insecurities, and needs—because I was more whole.

Finally, in addition to slowing down and working with our wounds, through our wandering back to our hearts we learn the vocational necessity of paying attention to passion. The passion to give our gift to the world often gets suppressed early in life. Parents or professors or bosses point us to the more practical matters of making money and building a career. And we go along with it. After all, it's what everyone else seems to be doing.

During the journey to get your heart back, however, the cooling embers within you get regathered, flames begin to flicker, and your desire grows to express your passion, to give your gift. It becomes, as the Hebrew prophet Jeremiah declares, like *a burning fire shut up in your bones.* You can't *not* express your calling. You can't *not* give your gift. You must find a way.

This is the profound challenge and burden of returning

home with your treasure. Once you're aware of it, you cannot un-know what you've discovered. You become haunted. Not by ambition or drive, but by the clear vision of who you are and why you're here. As you begin to take steps toward pursuing your passion, you are constantly presented with a choice: to fulfill your dream or to abandon it forever.

This is a great dilemma:

If you do nothing, it will be agonizing.

If you do something, it will be grueling.

Bringing It All Back Home

On the night before our escape from the canyon, after our final dinner together, we gathered for one last ceremony. We each were invited to tell the story of who we were when we descended into the canyon, who we had become during our time there, and what we were bringing back to our people. It wasn't about *explaining,* it was about storytelling and embodiment.

As we sat around the fire, each person took a turn, dramatizing our experiences in our own unique way. One participant shared a song that a mysterious woman by a river had sung to her in a dream. A man became the earth and wept for the harm caused by the human family. Dr. Neil howled like a wolf—a familiar sound I had heard in the distance during my solo. The ceremony was serious, but it was also strange and playful.

When it was my turn, I brought out my sarong one last time, covered my head, and became a jaguar. I entered the jungle with caution and curiosity. I listened to the sounds and watched the trees. I forged my own path and roamed across vast distances.

Everywhere I went the rainforest became lusher and more alive. Then I transfigured into the eternal man I had become when I faced my death beneath the ponderosa pines. I sang and spoke and uttered indiscernible sounds. I moved my hands delicately through the air and communicated a story of dead things coming back to life, of the hidden hummingbird hatchling, and of my own rebirth and taking flight and riding on the wind.

Others witnessed the story, but it wasn't for anyone else but me. The story came from my soul and it was in the language of my soul. It spoke the secret name that the wind whispered to me and it was an image that I could carry forward into everyday life as a celebration of all that transpired across the five canyon years of my life. It was an expression of what will always remain largely unutterable for every one of us—the gift that we each are, the gift that we hold to give to the world.

Under the night stars, we witnessed one another's stories and watched the embers fade. It was a night to sit in gratitude. But we would soon be faced with the hero's final difficult task:

> How do you give shape in the world to a sacred mystery that is beyond form?
> How do you translate into speech and action a transcendent truth?
> How do you deliver the contents of an uncontainable gift?

This is the question that follows the discovery of what your gift is, the question of how to bring it back home. Expression of your vocation is always an act of translation. In a job. In a moment. In a community. We will look at vocation through these lenses, but let's start with the most helpful place to begin translating your treasure: projects.

The Power of Projects

In the last chapter, we discussed how returning home calls for Ritual Practices, discernment in relationships, and decisive action in certain areas of our life. These are all relevant for sorting out vocational matters too. In addition to these endeavors, the guides encouraged us to take on a project (or projects) as a critical part of learning to translate our vocation in the world.

Projects are a powerful form of vocational expression for multiple reasons.

Most fundamentally, a project is a way of carrying forward what you found in your Leaving and Falling. It is a form of expressing who you have become with your reclaimed heart. Projects integrate your true identity from the dark, wild canyon-lands of soul with the realities of ordinary life.

You might plant a garden, make art, learn to play the piano, or study a new language. You might start coaching volleyball or volunteering for a local organization. After his first soul quest, our guide Knight picked up beekeeping. Interestingly, he advised, "Your project is probably something new that hasn't already been on your list." It is a fresh expression, emerging out of your full self.

Additionally, projects give the ego experience in serving the soul. In your previous life, your soul was suppressed and your Impostor had its way. As a persona the Impostor was really a distorted form of self put forward by ego. It was playing an outsized role, taking on too much responsibility. But now ego is no longer welcome in its Impostor forms—we've discharged those. Ego, however, is not only welcome, it is needed in its right-sized form, which is in service to soul. It is your X serving your Y. Ego plays a critical role in translating or delivering the mysteries of soul into the everyday world. It helps soul take shape and form through its capabilities of planning, designing, choosing, organizing, and coordinating. It also takes care of all of the email.

There is no one-size-fits-all approach to projects, which makes them the ideal vehicle for cultivating the proper soul-ego relationship. A project may be short-term, challenging your ego's proclivity to want to possess something or over-identify with a role or task. Or a project may be massive and life-sized—something you might never fully live into—challenging your ego's fears of achievement or commitment or perseverance. If the nature or format of a potential project challenges your previous operating system, then it is most likely a project you are being invited to undertake.

Lastly, a project brings focus. It is not uncommon to emerge from a soul journey with huge questions about your work, job, and career. Rather than waiting to sort out these larger, longer-term questions, projects enable you to get started, to experiment. They allow you to try on different ways of expressing your gift, independent of the bigger life decisions you may eventually have to make. Projects also keep you from returning to the surface of your life too quickly and making rash decisions about the questions you are holding. They facilitate a gentler re-entry and keep you from getting ill with the bends like a hasty deep sea diver coming up too fast.

The words of Spanish poet Antonio Machado are helpful here: *se hace camino al andar.* You make the way by walking. Projects generate momentum, helping you become more comfortable with risk by taking tangible actions instead of delaying for the kind of "clarity" that can remain ever-elusive.

I didn't know the specifics of my projects when I left the canyon. But soon after I returned, things began to crystallize. The first project came to me as I sat at a coffee shop one morning. I knew I needed to tell my story. I needed to show my true face and speak with my true voice. I decided that I would rent out a small neighborhood theater and find a creative way to give all that I had experienced in my Leaving, Falling, and Rising as a gift to my community. I would talk about the mystical moments in my life, simultaneously the most ridiculous and most sacred experiences. I wanted to help others awaken to these moments in their own past, present, and future. Because, ultimately, in a way that was consistent with the gift that I always sensed was mine to give, I wanted to help others live full-hearted lives, unearth the treasures of their calling, and share these gifts with one another and the world.

My project would take the form of a one-man show—part sermon, part standup comedy, part performance art.

I would only perform it once.

I wasn't going to make it into a thing.

I wasn't going to wrap my identity up in it.

I would create for the pure joy of creating.

I would give my gift wholeheartedly.

Calling and Career

These days there is a lot of pressure around having total alignment between your passion and the work you get paid to do.

People have high expectations that their jobs and careers should be places where they find deep fulfillment.

For a long time, I didn't think there was any other way. Getting paid to do my passion was all I knew (even if the pay wasn't very good!). Leading a spiritual community and neighborhood organizing were vehicles that helped me live out my calling. But then the community and organizational needs changed, and I changed too. I had to leave in order to find my heart and rediscover my vocation.

I also needed to pay the bills. So I took on a job that had some overlap with my vocation (remember the job that I had wanted to leave for four years?), but as it went on, I felt increasingly trapped. This is what I often wrestled with in my spiritual direction sessions with Tall Tim. *I've lost sense of my calling. I don't know what it is, but I know it's not this job. I want out. And yet what else would I even do?*

In all those walks around the lake, Tall Tim helped me see my preoccupation with my occupation. He helped slowly overcome the need to express my calling in my job. Once I gave up that obsession—which had a lot to do with how I knotted up my identity and worth with the roles I held and the work I did—I became a better listener to my life and more patient with the process of discovering and delivering my true powers.

There are seasons of life where your vocation and your job might overlap significantly. But there are also times where the substance or subject of your work couldn't feel further from the gift you bring to the world. It's important not to become rigidly attached to the idea that these two things must be the same thing. Conflating career with calling can hinder your growth, as it did for me.

In *Soulcraft*, Bill Plotkin shares Harley SwiftDeer's helpful framework for understanding how our vocation relates to our work, job, or career.

There is a survival dance.

And a sacred dance.

We all have to learn our *survival dance*. It's what pays the bills. It's how we support self and others. It's a necessary part of being a responsible human.

We all have a *sacred dance* too. It is a person's unique vocation. It is the Japanese concept of *ikigai*—a person's *reason for being* or *life purpose*. It is about carrying forward your treasure into the world. Projects are one way to develop this sacred dance. We also carry out this sacred dance in so many other areas of life, with family and friends, in hobbies, and through service and volunteering in local schools, sports, faith communities, and other organizations.

The survival dance is about making a living.

The sacred dance is about making a life.

Sometimes we might even get to do our sacred dance *as* our survival dance. To move toward a single, unified dance that expresses our sacred gift and covers our basic needs, says Plotkin, we must find or develop a viable delivery system. This vocational vehicle is a practical way of delivering our gift in the world. It is about balancing the pure essence of the calling with an accessible form. It is considerate of both the *content* and the *container*. Too much concern for the container and the content will be corrupted, no longer true to our calling. Too much concern for the content and our gifts will remain ungiven, sitting unused and ineffective on the warehouse shelves.

Once a vocational vehicle has been found or perhaps adapted, it is helpful to take on the mindset of an apprentice. There are skills to learn, certifications to receive, mentorships to seek out, side projects to work on, and relationships to form—all of which will assist in transforming the abstract aspects of your calling into the relevant forms the world is ready to receive. Over time, this process will evolve your sacred dance into what is also a sustainable survival dance.

I felt far from this reality. The role of neighborhood pastor had once worked as a vehicle for my calling. But it didn't anymore. I knew I wanted to continue to tend to matters of spirituality, community, and social impact, but I would need another culturally viable form to carry out that work. Something more expansive and open. So I began an apprenticeship with an emerging option. As my own meditation practice deepened, I came across the opportunity to become a certified meditation teacher. I also cleared a major hurdle—I stopped waiting for something to change with my job. And I started to create on the side. As an expression of my sacred dance, I started a pop-up event series called *Still Life*, bringing people together for community, music, poetry, and meditation. None of this was yet a job. I wasn't making any money. But it was deeply fulfilling because I was finding and developing creative ways to give my gift.

My quest brought me back to a parallel expression of the work I had always done, but I felt like a different person doing it. I was more whole. Likewise, whether your quest leads you into an entirely new discipline or career or brings you full circle—right back to the same desk in the same office in the same company where your journey started—you will be a fuller, freer version of yourself.

The Dharma Initiative

Work gets a lot of attention when it comes to considering calling. But it's important to remember that vocation is much more dynamic than a job or career.

The Hindu concept of dharma (which differs from some Buddhist understandings) provides insightful guidance here. The Sanskrit word *dharma* has many meanings, according to translator of Indian spiritual texts Eknath Easwaran, but at its core is the idea of "that which supports." Dharma is that which supports something from within—its essence, its virtue, its nature. Dharma's relationship to calling is evident here:

Dharma is what a thing is all about.

And what a thing is all about is its calling, its vocation.

It is with this meaning in mind that dharma is often understood to mean "purpose." But Vedic meditation teacher Thom Knoles cautions about the more fixed connotations that often come with this meaning. Dharma is much more exciting and interesting than just a single, consistent expression throughout our lives. A more accurate translation of dharma, Knoles teaches in his *Vedic Worldview* podcast, is *your personal role in the evolution of things.* It is about expressing your highest and best self, not just through a job or role. But in each moment.

Year by year.

Day by day.

Minute by minute.

To give your gift in the most generative way means that you are vigilantly attuned to what is being asked of you in each moment. You don't approach the world with a set agenda. Your contribution adapts and changes depending upon the circumstances and context.

This kind of dynamic expression of vocation isn't about *reacting* to the shifting expectations on the surface of life. Instead, it is about *responding* to *the sound of the genuine* in each moment. By being internally referenced to soul and source, you can deliver what a moment most critically needs from you.

This doesn't mean we can't come up with plans, or even build a skill set as we move toward a particular type of delivery system. But it does require that we stay flexible and open.

Author Steven Pressfield captures this kind of generous non-attachment in his book, *The War of Art,* suggesting that we ought to approach the creative process like a new mother, asking, "What do I feel growing inside me? Let me bring that forth, if I can, for its own sake and not for what it can do for me or how it can advance my standing."

After returning from the canyon, I approached more moments in my life with this kind of dynamic, creative spirit. I started to become attuned and responsive to each moment, experiencing a new calmness and presence in all of my endeavors. Genuine service replaced any anxious desire to impress or perform. I had sharpened senses that equipped me to spontaneously support people. I expressed care and concern for my colleagues in new ways. It was like I got out of the way of myself. More precisely, *my Impostor got out of the way* of my real self.

And You Give Yourself Away

In what has always been my favorite description of calling, author Frederick Buechner writes in *Wishful Thinking* that your vocation is "the place where your deep gladness and the world's deep hunger meet."

These words land us in what is the most important aspect of vocation to remember: Vocation, at its core, is about belonging to the human family and serving the world. In fact, the entire journey of getting your heart back is about becoming a more whole and healing presence in the world. You seek your true self to serve your community.

If the quest doesn't lead you into serving the human family and planet, then you still haven't retrieved your heart. You've settled for something else. You've refused to surrender. Because the common destination for anyone who has traveled this path is a life that radiates outward in tangible love to others—loved ones and rejected ones, neighbors and strangers, friends and enemies. The quest doesn't lead you to escape the world, but rather brings us all the way back home and immerses us fully in its complexities and challenges.

Your own rebirth plunges you into participation in the rebirth of all things. One Jewish mystical tradition calls this common human vocation *tikkun olam*, Hebrew for "repairing the world." This work of world repair is vast and varied. It calls for humans to end suffering wherever it is, to be healing agents across all spheres of life—personal, communal, social, and environmental.

Some repairers are called to the accompaniment of individuals, offering them nourishing support so that they may be more whole. Others are called to repair at the interpersonal or relational level, which involves cultivating belonging, peacebuilding, and reconciliation. Still others focus their repair efforts on a broader scale, working for equity, justice, and healing at systemic levels in institutions and society. And repairing the world is not just related to humans. Some answer the urgent call to be healers at an environmental or planetary level, restoring relationships between humans and the more than human world of plants, animals, and ecosystems—the jaguar at the zoo, the barred owl in the woods, the saguaro cactus in the desert.

When people undertake the arduous adventure of reclaiming their heart, it results in creative contributions beyond the existing cookie-cutter approaches in all of these areas. But even as adaptive approaches and innovative upgrades emerge from people pursuing their purpose, it is also the case that people give their gifts in profoundly ordinary ways. As stated at the outset of this chapter, this journey doesn't necessarily lead to flashy success. Countless full-hearted lives are quiet, but making extraordinary contributions under the radar in families, neighborhoods, and schools, across all levels of companies and organizations, and in bustling population centers and the most remote corners of the world.

The contexts for service are many, but the reality of the world's "deep need" cries out urgently for people to get their hearts back.

Mister Mystical

Six months after I returned from the quest, I stepped out onto the stage of a small local theater just down the street from Nayla's zoo. It was my birthday and I had invited my community to a weird one-man show.

It was my post-quest project.

It was called *Mister Mystical*.

It was an exploration of the mysteries, challenges, and joys of being human. It traced the same stories that appear in the pages of this book.

Of course, Cherie was there. Nico surprised me from southern California. My quest partner Dr. Neil came up from Oakland. Vanya and Tall Tim were there too. In front of these and other beloved friends, I revisited my dreams and re-met the wild creatures that had been my guides.

I raised provocative questions for the audience to consider in their own lives.

People told me that it stirred deep longings within them. That it made them think about their lives. About who they are and why they are here.

I was, of course, delighted to hear their feedback. But mostly, I was grateful. I had given my gift in a particular way. It was heart-forward and creative, authentic and elevating. It wasn't their response that was fulfilling, but that I had offered myself wholeheartedly back to the world.

As people stood and clapped and cheered at the show's conclusion, I had this sense that even though I'd had to travel vast inner distances to find this treasure, it had been with me the entire time.

The treasure was always *me*.

It was always *to love and be loved*.

It was always *that I belonged to these people and to the entire world*.

"Hold to your own truth at the center
of the image you were born with."

—David Whyte, "All the True Vows"

"His personal ambitions being totally
dissolved, he no longer tries to live
but willingly relaxes to whatever may
come to pass in him; he becomes,
that is to say, an anonymity."

—Joseph Campbell,
The Hero with a Thousand Faces

9

BE STILL

I Dream of Donald

Every year my three brothers and I choose a city and meet up there from the various places we live around the country for a weekend together. Away from our family responsibilities, we have time to catch up on life, laugh until we lose our voices, and enjoy good food and drink, board games, karaoke, and usually a sporting event. We get to be brothers again.

Being alone and hungry in that cold canyon was a stark contrast from these brothers' weekends, but that didn't mean these trips were far from my imagination. For most of the quest experience, my dreams were mellow. Even as I asked the dreammaker each night and prepared myself to receive something with my journal and pen next to my sleeping bag, my dreams remained faint and forgettable. Until one night—the first night of my solo—a deep dream finally came to me, and it brought me to an imaginary weekend reunion with my brothers.

We are in New York City together, standing and talking outside of a skyscraper. It's Trump Tower. One of my brothers gets a phone call and we're invited to go up to Trump's private penthouse. I'm not at all interested—thank you very much—but we decide to go.

We ride the elevator up and enter Trump's penthouse. More specifically, it is the same exact penthouse that belongs to the rich and cruel almanac-owning 1985 Biff Tannen from Back to the Future Part II. *It has chandeliers, faux gold stuff everywhere, jaguar and/or leopard print furniture, and a jacuzzi that seems like it's in the main room.*

Trump is there. He is mingling with other guests. I lose track of my brothers, but I sit down on the other side of the room, keeping my distance. I want nothing to do with him—this vile man who has locked children in cages, sexually assaulted dozens of women, called white supremacists "very fine people," withdrawn from global climate agreements, removed protections for endangered species, mocked a disabled reporter, called places "shithole countries," scammed hardworking contractors, formed a corrupt administration, bullied and gaslit a nation, and told a million lies (and who would go on to attempt a coup and commit countless other atrocities). In my mind, Trump is evil incarnate. I'm in the devil's lair. Sitting on a couch. Saying nothing. Watching from a distance.

But suddenly a large door opens. A little girl, four or five years old, enters the room. It's his granddaughter and she is beaming. I see them lock eyes. And I see his face become transfigured. From smug and insecure to tender and caring. She sprints to Trump. He crouches down, scoops her into his arms, and gives her a massive hug that she eagerly absorbs. The pair are squealing and giggling with delight.

I see kindness and gentleness.

I see light and love.

I see a radiant human being, who is worthy of love and has so much love to give.

Something inside of me breaks open as I witness this scene.

It's my heart.

My heart breaks open because it's as if I'm seeing the world through a new lens—the lens of pure love—for the first time.

Overwhelming love is flowing through me as I sit on the couch across the room, and I know I need to do something. I need to channel this love in some way. That's when I realize that I have a specific gift to give Trump—I have a song to sing for him.

I rise from my seat and approach him. And then I hug him. He's surprised, particularly because he had noticed I was keeping my distance from him.

"I have a gift for you," I say.

"Really? For me?" he asks excitedly with an innocent, bashful look on his face.

"I'm going to sing you your favorite song."

A smile spreads across his face as he chuckles with delight.

I drape one arm over his shoulder, begin to playfully dance, and sing:

"Start spreading the news!"

I proceed to belt out a rousing rendition of Frank Sinatra's version of the classic song "New York, New York."

Trump joins in. My brothers do too. We're singing, laughing, dancing, loving.

But then I wake up. I'm jolted out of this fantastical scene.

I'm in the middle of nowhere.

I'm alone, cold, and hungry.

And, I realize before I drift back to sleep, I'm kind of pissed off.

Because I've been off the grid for over a week—off Twitter and beyond the reach of Trump and his toxicity—but I still can't get away from this fucking asshole!

Lesson of Love

In the years preceding this dream, I encountered the jaguar and the owl, the saguaro and the sacred stones in a clearing. Poetry and *spots of time* and soul friends accompanied me along the way. And the day after serenading Trump, I would sing in the canyon and walk through the years of my life, before returning home to the kind welcome of family, and new possibilities. This Donald dream was an echo of all that came before and all that would follow.

It was disturbing, but it was enlightening.

It worked on me in strange ways.

As the days went on, I realized it wasn't just a dream.

It was a vision.

Because it sealed a message into my soul.

The message of the dream?

The message of getting your heart back?

The message?

It is something so elemental, printed on the most basic greeting card and sung in the cheesiest pop song.

And yet something so magnificent and inexpressible, pointed to by the mystics in poetry, story, and song across the ages.

It is the Leaving, the Falling, the Rising.

It is the path, the journey, the destination.

It is the true treasure of the quest—the source of *the sound of the genuine* and the one and only human vocation.

The message is love.

Love. Love. Love.

Life is all about love.

Immeasurable, unconditional love.

Love is our essence. It is where we come from. It is our destiny.

Love is who I am and why I'm here.

Love is who you are and why you're here.

Love is who we all are and why we're all here.

It is one thing to learn this lesson in the company of kind creatures, generous landscapes, and compassionate community. But an even more terrible and wonderful revelation to receive in the faux gold penthouse of your enemy. An ancient Hebrew songwriter wrestled with this omnipresent, inescapable nature of love:

Where can I flee from your presence?
If I go up to the heavens, you are there;
if I make my bed in the depths, you are there.

The vision showed me that *love is an absurd, unstoppable force.* There's nothing beyond its reach, even the most horrible, hateful tyrant. In the presence of a symbol of pure evil, my eyes were opened and I could see a "child of God," one whose core identity is *beloved.* And it called forth from me even more love in the form of a gift, a song.

This is what happens when you get your heart back: you can't help but *see through the lens of love.*

As Brené Brown puts it in *Braving the Wilderness,* you gain the capacity to find the face of God in everyone you meet. That includes power-hoarding politicians, fear-mongering media figures, Twitter trolls, and anyone whose views are the antithesis of what you stand for. "When we desecrate their divinity, we desecrate our own," she writes.

You start to answer and embody an emphatic *yes* to the question Victor Hugo asks in *Les Miserables*: "Is there not in every human soul, a primitive spark, a divine element, incorruptible in this world and immortal in the next, which can be developed by goodness, kindled, lit up, and made to radiate, and which evil can never entirely extinguish?"

This story is true, you realize.

True of those who have forgotten, ignored, and rejected you.

True of those who have carved your wounds.

True of those who have harmed and hated you and your people and other people.

True of those who you think are undeserving.

Love has always been their fundamental identity.

It's just that they forgot their way.

They became estranged from their true selves.

They lost their hearts.

Just like you and me.

Master of the Two Worlds

I came back from the canyon years of my life with the general reintegration issues and the specific vocational concerns, but this revelation was the biggest burden. It was an expansive vision. The deepest truth.

No big deal, right?

The transcendent vision of Prince Arjuna in the *Bhagavad Gita*, in which he witnessed his charioteer Krishna in his eternal form as Vishnu, Lord of the Universe, left him trembling and stammering. Likewise, the vision of all-encompassing, abundant love delivered to me in the Donald dream and a myriad of other mystical moments was *glorious*. Specifically, it was glorious in the Hebrew sense of the word. The root of the Hebrew word for glory—*kabod*—means *heavy, weighty*. It shook me. It challenged me. It left me with serious questions about how to steward this knowledge:

> *How do I remember this?*
> *How do I integrate this reality into my life?*
> *How do I live now?*

The thousand-year-old story told in the *Ten Oxherding Pictures* and its accompanying poems provide guidance about how to handle this weighty task. The Zen story, which has been adapted over time, chronicles the journey of the young ox-herder who ventures out into the distant mountains to find an ox. He eventually recovers and tames the ox. After he brings the ox home, he experiences a sublime vision in which *everything* merges together into *nothing*—whip, rope, person, ox. The herder has encountered the source of everything (which is what the entire search for the ox is a parable about). But rather than remain in the extraordinary, he returns to the ordinary.

The final picture, along with this poem, portrays this experience of reintegrating with society:

> *Barefooted and naked of breast,*
> *I mingle with the people of the world.*
> *My clothes are ragged and dust-laden,*
> *and I am ever blissful.*
> *I use no magic to extend my life;*

Now, before me, the dead trees
become alive.

Blissful in the *ragged.*
Alive in the *dead.*
Two worlds *mingling . . .*
This characterizes what follows your Leaving, Falling, and Rising. Campbell calls this the experience of becoming a Master of the Two Worlds. Let's call these two worlds the realm of love and the realm of the everyday.

Most people have the problem of forgetting our belonging to the realm of love—that's why we have to journey home in the first place. But the reverse problem can surface when we return—we can forget our belonging to the realm of the everyday.

When this happens, our newfound non-attachment deteriorates into detachment.

Detachment is aloof. It is a state of being emotionally distant and disengaged from reality. It can be self-absorbed, lacking concern and care for others. It can be self-righteous, holding a *holier than thou* attitude.

Non-attachment, meanwhile, is the result of letting go of false identities, demanding expectations, and grasping ambitions. It is not anxious or selfish or clingy. It is a relaxed and open state. Non-attachment is rooted in love and engages the world through presence, humility, curiosity, and gratitude. It recognizes that we belong to a much bigger story.

To be a Master of the Two Worlds—or what Einstein called a *genius in the art of living*—means fostering a flowing, dynamic connection between the realm of love and the realm of the everyday. Instead of leading to detached withdrawal, exposure to the realm of love becomes an animating force in the realm of the everyday. It guides our presence, relationships, and work. And as we engage the realm of the everyday, we don't get stuck, but return to the realm of love for grounding and nourishment. We flow between our awareness of the unity and oneness of everything and the particularities of a moment and the distinct contribution that is ours to make.

We cannot afford to escape the realm of the everyday—no matter how callous it is with its patterns of self-preservation and cowardice, insatiable greed and senseless violence, power-hoarding and fearmongering, ecological abuse and dehumanization, endless consumption and numbing distractions.

We can't disregard these realities and disappear into love.

Because there are so many challenges right in front of us that demand our action.

And besides, then it isn't truly love anymore.

It's indifference.

In fact, the relentless love encountered on the quest is not soft and delicate. It is sharp and strong. It's a force to be reckoned with. Even as it declares that everyone belongs and is beloved, that no one is beyond its reach—including hateful tyrants in penthouses whose favorite song may or may not actually be "New York, New York"—love also fiercely demands change and calls for accountability.

Love converts outrage into empathy.

Love works for justice and equity.

Love resists what divides and destroys.

Love establishes boundaries to promote healing and growth.

As one ancient spiritual teacher wrote, love tells the truth, it protects, it perseveres. *Love never fails.*

To be a Master of the Two Worlds is to be a creative conduit of this transforming, renewing, restoring love in everyday life.

It is to express the eternal in the everyday.

It is to be still.

The Movement of Stillness

As I traversed these rugged years of my life, my desired destination frequently shifted. I wanted to live somewhere else. I wanted to travel around the world. I wanted a new job. Usually, behind whatever I wanted was a desire for either security or novelty, depending on the mood I was in. But most often, I craved clarity. I just wanted to know what was next. I wanted some certainty about what to do.

I never arrived at clarity or certainty.

Instead, I found stillness.

Stillness is most often thought of along the lines of its common definition, *the absence of movement or sound*. Stillness is motionless. Stillness is silent.

But this definition falls short when it comes to practicing stillness in our lives. It's only half of the story. Because stillness cannot be fully understood in isolation. It is a cause that always comes with an effect. Everything that surrounds stillness carries its signature. It is known not only in *being*, but also in *moving* and *going* and *doing*.

As travel writer Pico Iyer observes in *The Art of Stillness*, "The point of gathering stillness is not to enrich the sanctuary or mountaintop but to bring that calm into the motion, the commotion of the world."

In other words, stillness *moves*.

From pause to activity.

Essence to form.

Retreat to return.

From the wilderness to the city.

Solitude to community.

Contemplation to action.

Stillness is the superpower that enables us to move back and forth between the realm of love and the realm of the everyday.

As my Ritual Practices expanded and deepened over the years, my capacity to carry stillness forward into the rest of my life increased. Experience taught me another elemental truth about stillness:

Stillness is the centered place between striving and squandering.

To strive is to reach anxiously into the future—demanding clarity, grabbing at control, attaching to outcomes. Striving worships success. It tries to play God.

To squander is to slip away into the past. Squandering is stagnant. It refuses to carry out a calling. It runs from risk, fears failure, and stays away from sacrifice. Squandering buries treasure.

But stillness is the narrow way between these two approaches to life. Stillness remains in the here and now. The unknown is its playground. Change is its friend. It is no stranger to surrender. Stillness is grateful for what has been and welcomes what is to come. It cooperates with the flow of life.

It's common to get lost in striving or squandering. To vacillate between them or to plunge fully into one posture. For a long time, striving was my default mode of operation. It is what governed my Impostor's pursuit of productivity, perfection, and the approval of others. Even after I left my Impostor behind, striving kept me asking for clarity, certainty, and security. It had me chasing after some future "happiness" as if the next thing would satisfy and complete me (which, of course, it never does).

But stillness gave me more than these elusive pursuits ever could.

Stillness awakened me again and again to the present moment.

And in the present, I found contentment.

In the present, I discovered *I always have my heart.*

Meditation

It was especially the practice of meditation that instilled stillness into my life. I had engaged many approaches to contemplation and mindfulness over the years, but after my wilderness quest, I felt pulled to deepen my meditation practice. As I mentioned, I began to close my eyes in meditation for twenty minutes twice a day and soon I noticed how different my experience of life was becoming when my eyes were open.

Meditation is a term used to refer to a wide range of different practices from various religious and cultural traditions. The word comes from the Latin *meditari* meaning *to contemplate* or *to ponder.* This definition accurately reflects meditation techniques that involve focusing or concentrating on something, such as a phrase, the breath, a person, the name of a divine being, or the content of one's thoughts. But this doesn't describe all meditation styles. Another genre of meditation, including one of the earliest known forms of meditation that emerged in ancient India, focuses on *moving beyond focus.*

Instead of clinging to or judging thoughts, this type of meditation involves gently moving through thoughts and settling into a deep form of relaxation of mind and body. It is a way to access inner stillness. The result is feeling more present, connected, and adaptable in relationship to all of life.

Practicing this style of meditation was a game-changer for me. It felt like it took all the benefits I had experienced through my other Ritual Practices and Mystical Presence and established them as my permanent way of being. Instead of running on the fear, anxiety, self-absorption, and comparison of striving, I began to run on a completely different energy. It was the cleaner, heart-driven energy of stillness. No more fight, flight, or freeze. I found flow.

There are many meditation options, and these different avenues are worth exploring in order to find a technique that helps you stabilize stillness as a way of life. Choose what works for you, but choose something! Because if you don't choose the object of your meditation—whether it involves focusing on something nourishing, or moving beyond focus into stillness—it will choose you. As Joseph Campbell once said, "All of life is a meditation, most of it unintentional."

Unintentional meditation takes over when we don't actively cultivate intention in our lives. We likely end up fixated on some surface situation or physical condition—making more money, possessing more things, accomplishing more at work, acquiring power, growing influence, attracting sexual interest, micromanaging the lives of our children. Without *intention*, our *attention* moves away from the heart and into these other areas.

Many have said, *where your attention goes, your energy flows.* This means attention determines a lot about our lives, which makes it one of our most powerful assets. Tragically, every day we are bombarded with ads, promotions, alarms, and notifications that are trying to steal away our attention—and they are very successful! The result is deterioration in so many areas of our lives, such as creativity, communication, and contentment. So meditation isn't some tame, humble activity; it is an act of rebellion against the nonstop campaign to manipulate and control your attention. It is a way to protect your power. Meditation is about curating the kind of life you want to live—what you want to concentrate on and carry forward, and what you want to leave behind.

Unintentional meditation is about living from the outside in.

Intentional meditation is about living from the inside out.

Ultimately, *intentional* meditation that directs your *attention* isn't just about where your energy flows.

It's about who you become.

Who you are.

The *Brihadaranyaka Upanishad* declared this truth almost three thousand years ago:

You are what your deep, driving desire is.

As your desire is, so is your will.

As your will is, so is your deed.

As your deed is, so is your destiny.

If you want your heart, you will keep it. If you seek stillness, you will find it. If your allegiance is to love, you will become it.

Meditation is my gateway to stillness. Twice a day, I enter and I remember my connectedness to all things. I am reminded of who I am and why I am here. I return to love, and I'm recharged to live this love daily.

In other words, meditation is how I get my heart back.

Every day.

Follow Your Bliss

I'm not sure when it happened. There probably wasn't even a specific moment. But at some point I knew that I had completed my quest to get my heart back, including the final phase of Rising to my new self.

Of course, the work of giving my gift would be ongoing—it continues even as I write these words—but I was already experiencing the bounty of what I had recovered overflowing across the different areas of my life. In performing the one-man show and hosting the community meditation events. In bringing a different ease and kindness into my job. In leading others on Wanders in the wild and together with Cherie taking our son on a mini-quest and rite of passage for his tenth birthday. In speaking and teaching opportunities that came my way. And in all sorts of ordinary interactions.

Authenticity marked my presence. I was no longer obsessed with outcomes. My concern was to be fully present to the people I was with and to bless them in any way I could. I was open and adaptable, not planning out the future, but always listening to life and trying to respond to the next right thing. And as I was faithful to where life had led me, I noticed that different connections, opportunities, and resources started coming my way.

I suppose, as Joseph Campbell would say, I was *following my bliss*.

In his famous PBS interview with Bill Moyers and its book form *The Power of Myth*, Campbell discusses a Sanskrit phrase that represents "the jumping-off place to the ocean of transcendence": *sat, chit, ananda*. He translates them as *being, consciousness*, and *bliss*.

Focusing on the final term, Campbell explains, "If you follow your bliss, you put yourself on a kind of track that has been there all the while, waiting for you, and the life that you ought to be living is the one you are living . . . Wherever you are—if you are following your bliss, you are enjoying that refreshment, that life within you, all the time."

Follow your bliss became a catchphrase for Campbell's work.

Following your bliss is about finding deep fulfillment in the gift of life.

Bliss is the freedom and joy you experience when you no longer let your Impostor live your life. Bliss is your experience of the world when you are anchored in stillness—overflowing with gratitude and wonder, and actively contributing to the repair of the world. When you embody your sacred dance, you are following your bliss.

It is not a selfish or impulsive endeavor.

It's not easy or noncommittal.

It's not superficial or escapist.

To follow your bliss is to prioritize the growth of your inner life rather than obsessing over the outer details. It is to live in a heart-forward way instead of chasing after certain goals or ambitions, requiring specific details or conditions, or demanding certainty or clarity about the future. "Follow your bliss and don't be afraid," said Campbell, "and doors will open where you didn't know they were going to be."

It means seeing and living your life as a life of *mythic* proportions. It means embracing the world as drenched in the *mystical*. It involves turning to Ritual Practices to keep you rooted in your true self.

To follow your bliss is to be still.

To follow your bliss is to get your heart back, to keep it, to give its abundant love away and away and away again.

Flying Onward

One ordinary day in late February 2020 I was out for an early morning jog, almost six years after the rainy morning when I realized I couldn't run anymore. I entered the nearby forest and descended on the trail into the ravine, continuing along the trickling stream where salmon die and are born, past the century-old red cedar stump and the place where I met the wise owl, and to a small platform overlooking the sea. My heart was pounding in my chest. I took a deep breath of the salty air and gazed out at the water below and the mountains beyond. I thought about the things I had to do that day and wondered about what the next year might hold. I was excited. I was open. But I had no idea what was coming. That a global pandemic was coming. That it had *already* quietly arrived.

Then, as I had done so many times before, I turned around and began my jog back home. A mile or two later, just as I was emerging from the forest and returning to the city streets, a hummingbird darted out in front of me. It danced in the air, hovering above my return trail for a few moments before dashing back into the woods. Immediately, I remembered the hatchling from my final morning in the canyon. I remembered the dead birds and the hawk feather that I had found on my wilderness quest. I remembered the pigeon shit and the owl encounter and the hummingbird my daughter released. And I remembered the secret name I was given on the edge of the cliff right after I said goodbye to my Impostor in the circle of stones in the valley below.

A great calamity was coming. Even still, I felt myself soaring to new heights. I was gliding through the sky toward a destination that I did not know. But not knowing didn't matter. I was fully alive. I was here. I was now. I had all that I needed to face whatever the next challenge might be, or the one after that.

I had my heart.

I had everything.

"We shall not cease from exploration
And the end of all our exploring
Will be to arrive where we started
And know the place for the first time."

—T.S. Eliot, "Little Gidding,"
from *Four Quartets*

"What, now, is the result of the
miraculous passage and return?"

—Joseph Campbell,
The Hero with a Thousand Faces

BEGIN AGAIN

Leaving Seattle

We were driving east into the mountains, away from the place that had been Cherie's and my home for fourteen years, the birthplace of our three children and the only home they had ever known. Tears were pouring down my face. I could barely utter a word.

We were moving.

Not even a month before, in the midst of the initial pandemic shutdown, we had made the decision to relocate two thousand miles across the country. We spent the week before our departure packing up our belongings. That morning we said farewell to our house. And just thirty minutes earlier we said our final goodbyes to our incredible friends. I had been crying ever since.

The tears actually started to gather earlier than that. Before the kids woke up that morning, I snuck out of the house for one last run through my favorite park. As I made one final visit to my *spot of time,* I finally started to be present to the emotions I hadn't made much space for in the previous month while we were dealing with all the moving logistics. The intensity of the feelings escalated from there.

As was the case so often during this journey, grief and gratitude were intermingled.

I was thrilled about the new opportunities for work, family, and home in front of us—things that a false, former part of me had fixated on for so long. But these possibilities were no longer in my imagination, they were in real life, where things come with a cost. The steep price we were paying was leaving the close-knit community that had become our family over the past decade. It was brutal (especially having to say goodbye during the pandemic) *and* it left me almost speechless with gratitude for all that we had shared across the years around kitchen tables and on front porches, at neighborhood parks and local bars, and in countless ordinary, day-to-day interactions.

A sense of awe was also behind my tears. At many points throughout the journey, I felt like surface conditions of my life were draining my energy and robbing me of my prime, as if they were my kryptonite. But eventually I realized that I wasn't becoming weaker, I was becoming stronger. The challenges were my fuel. They were growing my power. And now I was at full capacity, ready to weather whatever storms might come in this next season, and fully prepared to be present to my family as we endured trials and tribulations of this new adventure.

As we drove away, I was aware that this cross-country move wasn't just the end of an era in terms of where we lived. It also symbolized a clear ending to my inner journey. As grueling as the six years had been, and as much as I had wanted to speed through them at times, I couldn't help but feel a heavy sorrow now that it was ending. It caught me off guard. And yet I realized

I wasn't alone in this experience. I was reminded of a feature in Bill Plotkin's book *Nature and the Human Soul,* in which he explores eight life stages. I was a few chapters into the book when I noticed that he ends each chapter—*each stage of the life journey*—with an acknowledgment that essentially says, *you have a deep sadness that this part of your journey has come to an end. It was the best stage of life to be in.*

This whole journey was the best season of my life.

It really was.

Well, that is, besides the one after that, and the one after that, and the one after that . . .

A Life Full of Sequels

One of the first movies I remember seeing in the theater is *Back to the Future Part II,* the middle chapter of the famous Sci-Fi/Comedy/Adventure trilogy that made a supporting appearance in my Trump dream in the canyon. As soon as the movie started, I was intrigued because it opened with the same scene that the first movie ended with—except for the fact that Marty's girlfriend Jennifer was all the sudden played by actress Elisabeth Shue, who my third-grade self was majorly crushing on, but I digress . . . At any rate, in the duplicated scene, Doc Brown, inventor of the DeLorean time machine, blasts into the hero Marty's driveway in 1985 from the year 2015, just after Marty has returned home from his first adventure in 1955.

The end of the first movie is the beginning of the next.

Doc has come from the future with a new mission for Marty. A new challenge.

A new beginning.

There is an adventure. And then another adventure.

We see the same idea in the million Marvel movies.

And even much earlier in Homer's epics. *The Iliad* tells the story of the final year of the decade-long Trojan War. *The Odyssey* continues the story of one Greek warrior, chronicling the last six weeks of his ten-year journey home.

So it is also with the days of our lives. Christian tradition speaks of ending and beginning as a *daily* process that involves dying to old, limiting ways and rising to fresh, life-giving ones.

One mission is completed and another opens up.

One story ends and another one begins.

Life is full of sequels.

It constantly gives us opportunities to participate in the cycle of beginnings and endings so we can grow. Endings help us accrue wisdom and power to face new trials. Beginnings help us stay humble and open to ensure that we continue evolving and expanding.

Leaving Seattle represented the end of this particular journey of Leaving and Falling and Rising. It was also the start of a new story. We were answering an invitation to depart from life as we knew it. We needed help along the way. And for me, it was another opportunity to let go. To learn who I was beyond the place that had shaped me and been a major source of my identity for a decade and a half. To shed my Seattle identity. To put my hard-won stillness into action.

Beginning Again Together

It was a fascinating time to begin again. Because we were very obviously not alone.

Our own move was, in part, precipitated by the decisions of friends to say *Yes* to new beginnings in other places. It gave us courage to step into the next unknown chapter of our story. It was a domino effect.

As we moved deeper into the pandemic, we found ourselves surrounded by a sea of humanity that was also learning to start over. Life as we knew it had been shipwrecked. Loved ones lost, health and energy sapped, families and communities divided, jobs lost or altered, businesses destroyed. So much suffering.

And yet, amid the devastation, countless people began to experience more than just an interruption. They heard an invitation. They adopted new Ritual Practices. Solitude, creativity, body movement, even baking sourdough bread (sorry, Wordle doesn't count). Yes, there were also the challenges of binge watching, Zoom meetings, excessive drinking, and overeating, but so many people began to slow down. To get quiet. And they discovered what German theologian Dietrich Bonhoeffer named: "In silence is embedded the marvelous power of clarification, purification and concentration on essentials." In that silence they began to hear what they had been too busy to pay attention to before. They started to say *Yes* to the Call to Adventure that had been there all along.

Part of what the pandemic revealed at a massive scale is that so much of how we've arranged our lives just isn't sustainable. In fact, there's so much excess and so many distractions that we no longer want. We don't want to go back to the way things were. We want to integrate what we've discovered during this trying time. We want to live more authentic, present, and connected lives.

And even if this is a realization you have not yet personally had as a result of the pandemic catastrophe, perhaps you'll notice the cascading effects of new beginnings in the lives of those around you, and hear an invitation. It's not too late to hurl yourself into the soul quest and soak up all the life and love that awaits you there.

Stay Weird

In *A Religion of One's Own,* psychotherapist and ex-monk Thomas Moore recalls a story from the early 1970s. He was eating breakfast with an academic who was well-known but whose work on mythology had not yet become popular. It was Joseph Campbell, before he started to say, "Follow your bliss" when referring to listening to your inner life and following the signs to find and live your calling. Instead, during their lively conversation, Campbell used another term for the journey: *wyrd.*

Wyrd refers to an ancient image of a trio of sisters who spin the threads of fate. The term meant "having the power to control destiny," and that's exactly what the wyrd sisters did. Eventually, *wyrd* became *weird* and its meaning evolved into "unearthly" and, later, "odd, strange."

Before it became *Follow your bliss* it was *Be faithful to your wyrd,* or at least that's the phrase Campbell and Moore explored that morning over breakfast. It didn't ultimately make the cut, but I wonder if *Be faithful to your wyrd* is an even more helpful description for what it means to be someone who travels the way home, given *wyrd*'s various definitions:

The way is *odd*, in case you haven't figured it out already. You make *strange* choices and you do *strange* things that make you stand out from society.

The way is *unearthly*. You open yourself up to the mystical magic of the world.

The way is about *the power to control your destiny*. Rather than passively waiting for some fixed and predetermined life to happen to you, when you carry out this quest, you claim the power to participate in the unfolding of your life. You dance with the sacred. You live your legend. You make your myth.

To walk the way home is to *Be faithful to your wyrd*.

It is to *Stay Weird*.

And when you *Stay Weird*, your ability to respond and adapt to each new beginning becomes more and more effortless. Because you've got your heart and you've cultivated stillness.

As my meditation teacher—an *anam cara* of mine—said to me after a series of new beginnings in my life that included the chaos of a cross-country move, more pandemic challenges, and starting a new job and losing it a year and a half later, when you face new beginnings after already getting your heart back, it is like you rush into the cave to slay a dragon and you pull out your sword. But when you look up, you realize there is no monster! Because you've already slayed the big beast. Instead, when you face new trials you still need to go into the cave, but this time you just light a fire and read the wisdom on the walls to remind you of your way.

Once you get your heart back, you still face challenges, but much of their monstrous power has been diminished. You still have to navigate the dynamics of Leaving the familiar, Falling into the unknown, and Rising to wholeness, but you are equipped to do so with greater ease because you've become intimately acquainted with the pattern. Through whatever comes, you *Stay Weird*, guarding your heart from the million ways to lose it, learning what you need to learn, becoming who you are destined to become.

Hugging the Cactus

I stood naked on top of that small, unremarkable mountain in the Arizona desert. The saguaro cactus had just shared its gut-wrenching story with me. How it was stabbed. How it was shot (at least) four times. My face was soaked in tears.

I had followed a tiny butterfly to the saguaro. I had heeded its command to take off my clothes. And it had delivered on its promise to tell me its story. By this point, the rational, doubting, *hell-no-this-isn't-real* part of my mind that was resisting had completely shut up. The only thing that remained was the *all-in* part of me.

As I wiped away the tears, the cactus beckoned me, so I approached. For a moment, I stood naked next to it. I felt safe and connected in its presence. Noticing a rock at its base, I sat down carefully. Everything was silent, except for the sound of my breath. Then very slowly I wrapped my arms and legs around the prickly being.

And I hugged the cactus.

The embrace, I knew then, was an apology. For all the harm

the cactus—and the entire planet—has endured at the hands of humans.

And later I realized it was much more than this.

The hug was also a lament. For our estrangement from one another, and for the million ways we choose to lose our hearts.

The hug was a pledge too. That I would always *Stay Weird* and pursue my heart above all else.

The hug, finally, was an expression of gratitude.

For our sacred interaction—that the saguaro spoke to me, and I was foolish enough to listen. A sign that I was on my way home.

For all that had come before this moment—the invitation to get my heart back, the many kind companions and the luxury car slogan, the jaguar dream and the owl encounter, the circle of stones and the secret name. It was all real!

And for all the weird things that were yet to come—the quiet canyon where I walked through the years of my life and witnessed the hatched hummingbird, the struggles of my homecoming and the joys of stillness, and all the new beginnings and adventures that stretch into the future, far beyond the pages of this book.

Make Your Myth

Four empty bullet shells sit on my desk as I write these final words, souvenirs from my cactus encounter. A ponderosa pinecone sits on the windowsill nearby, recalling my death in the canyon. Around my office, which Nico affectionately calls my *cat cave,* are a greeting card featuring an owl, an elegant carved jaguar statue from Dr. Neil, and a decorative coffee mug my kids gave me that has a drawing of a prickly saguaro on it accompanied by the words "Can't touch this." There are many other weird objects too.

Perhaps it's obvious, but I surround myself with this collection of memorabilia to remind me of the sacred season of life that I traversed. It's not that I'm trying to relive the "glory days." It's because as I move into the future I want to constantly be reminded of my desire—and, more fundamentally, my calling—to live a soul-centered life. I want to hear the Call to Adventure that steadily reverberates deep within myself, a sound which so many other forces try to drown out.

But there is one other important lesson that is crystal clear when I look at these eclectic totems: *my myth is my own.* Even as my way home was an echo of a *universal* pattern, my journey was entirely *unique.* And so is yours.

Indeed this book has chronicled the twists and turns, the allies and foes, and the obstacles and open doors of my adventure. But my intention all along has been to equip you to *make your myth.*

Yes, imitate the grand pattern that countless wise ones have passed on to us. Use the map!

But, above all, as you embark on your healing journey, embrace the particularities of your story. The magical guides and nourishing practices. The devastating discoveries and generous teachers. The desolate places and enlightening dreams.

Welcome all of it.

Because if you listen to your life, you will always find your way home.

RITUAL PRACTICES
REFERENCE GUIDE

RESOURCES

Learn to meditate, get support for your journey, and stay connected with me at benjaminkatt.com.

For more Joseph Campbell, start with *The Power of Myth* and *The Hero with A Thousand Faces*

Anything by Bill Plotkin, but especially *Soulcraft*

The poetry of David Whyte, Mary Oliver, Rainer Maria Rilke, and any poet Pádraig Ó Tuama introduces you to in *Poetry Unbound: 50 Poems to Open Your World*; and the poetic blessings of John O'Donohue in *To Bless the Space Between Us*

For the old stories, see *Mythology: Timeless Tales of Gods and Heroes* by Edith Hamilton, *Norse Mythology* by Neil Gaiman, *Women Who Run with the Wolves* by Clarissa Pinkola Estés, and the soulful storytelling of Martin Shaw

Two of my favorite fictional legends: *The Lord of the Rings* trilogy by J.R.R. Tolkien and *The Alchemist* by Paulo Coelho

After Whiteness by Willie James Jennings for the Possession-Control-Mastery force and *Living Resistance* by Kaitlin Curtice on resisting it

Falling Upward by Richard Rohr and *The Middle Passage* by James Hollis on midlife

Rest Is Resistance by Tricia Hersey on rest

24/6 by Tiffany Shlain on technology and shabbat

The Power of Ritual by Casper ter Kuile on everyday rituals

Black Elk Speaks by John G. Neihardt for visions; *Memories, Dreams, Reflections* by Carl Jung for dreams; *King, Warrior, Magician, Lover* by Robert Moore and Douglas Gillette on masculine archetypes

The Awakened Brain by Lisa Miller on the neuroscience of spirituality

The War of Art by Steven Pressfield on creativity

Let Your Life Speak by Parker Palmer and *A Sacred Voice Is Calling* by John Neafsey on vocation

Learning to Walk in the Dark by Barbara Brown Taylor on darkness

The Dance of the Dissident Daughter by Sue Monk Kidd on evolving faith and *A Religion of One's Own* by Thomas Moore on spirituality

The Great Conversation by Belden Lane on nature and the soul

The Wild Edge of Sorrow by Francis Weller on grief

An Indomitable Beast: The Remarkable Journey of the Jaguar by Alan Rabinowitz on jaguars

Podcasts for your journey: *On Being* with Krista Tippett, *Unknowing* with Brie Stoner, *Poetry Unbound* with Pádraig Ó Tuama, and *Vedic Worldview* with Thom Knoles

Find a Spiritual Director at Spiritual Directors International, www .sdicompanions.org.

Descend into a wilderness quest with Animas Valley Institute, www.animas.org.

Join a community to nurture your spiritual life with The Nearness, www.thenearness.coop.

Explore the work of Joseph Campbell at the Joseph Campbell Foundation, www.jcf.org.

ACKNOWLEDGMENTS

There are a million people I want to thank—not only those who helped make this book possible, but also those who have supported me throughout all the different phases of my journey. This list is not comprehensive!

Thank you:

Joel Fotinos, for looking past my small platform and answering the call that this book issued to you; and the entire team at St. Martin's Essentials for your careful attention to this project.

Don Pape, for understanding the in-betweenness of this book in terms of spirituality and genre, and coming alongside me just when I needed a wise guide in the world of publishing.

Nico, for your restless pursuit of the Wild One—*it's all real*—and for always calling forth my jaguarness. I am who I am because you are who you are.

Casper ter Kuile, for introducing me to so many incredible people. The connections you've made have altered the course of my life.

Heather Stringer, for thinking of me and making a critical introduction at the exact hour I needed it.

My Seattle community, for all our creating, healing, and playing together. The Leavy crew, Awake, and Aurora Commons.

Matt and Chris, for your steady friendship and enthusiastic support through all the phases of this story and book. The Tigert family, for always being a refuge and for the world of ordinary moments we've shared.

Mom and Dad, for setting me on the way; for your abundant support. What a beautiful homecoming it has been! Bill, Dan, and Tim, for the annual adventures, everyday texts, laughter, karaoke, and encouragement. Being your brother is one of the most cherished gifts in my life.

The guides from different seasons of my life: the people of BCRC, Cherith and Nord, Randy, Ron, Rob, Christiana, Tall Tim, Vanya, Knight and Bear, Krista, and Jonni. Chris, for the out-of-nowhere invitation to Peru where I wrote almost a third of this book by hand in a hammock in the jungle. The host of "good kindnesses" I have encountered along the way, including but certainly not limited to Lout, Tim Soerens, Jay, Karen, Sparrow, Andy, Neil and the Animas initiates, Danya, 1 Giant Mind, cousin Elizabeth, and Lillie B.

The musicians who accompanied me during my writing: Nils Frahm, Ólafur Arnalds, and Luke Howard.

My beloved family, especially, for your generous support and encouragement as I wrote this book, even as most of it took place during the pandemic while we were all housebound and adjusting to a cross-country move.

Evie, for your overflowing passion for life. You remind me to stay awake to the glory of it all.

Jackson, for the attentive kindness you bring to everything. I want to be like you when I grow up.

Zara, for expressing the creative genius that flows through you. You teach me to be an artist.

Cherie, for the magical story we have been writing together across these years. I bless those young, innocent versions of us for finding one another, for engaging life as a grand adventure, and for encouraging each other's evolution. Thank you for prioritizing your heart. Thank you for cultivating and protecting the soul of our family. Thank you for believing in me. This book doesn't happen without your willingness to risk with me, to provide for us while I focused on this project, and to get the kids ready for school every day so I could write just a little longer. The words on these pages are mine, but this whole thing is *our* story.

ABOUT THE AUTHOR

Mouna Photography

BEN KATT is a meditation teacher and life transformation coach who has been leading, innovating, and inspiring at the intersection of spirituality, community, and social healing for almost twenty years. Previously, he led The On Being Project's work in supporting religious and spiritual leaders. He holds a Master of Divinity degree and was an ordained minister for more than a decade. Ben lives with his family in Milwaukee, Wisconsin.